The Universal Language

Poetry of Life, Light, and Love

SpiritMan

Copyright © 2018 by Benjamin H. Martin (Spirit Man). All rights reserved. No part of this book may be used or reproduced in any manner without written permission from the author except for the use of brief quotation in a book review or scholarly journal.

ISBN: 978-0-692-08888-3

Publisher
SpiritMan (Benjamin Martin)
www.spiritman222.com

Editing, formatting and cover design by
Williams DocuPrep
www.williamsdocuprep.com

Dedication

Reverend Benjamin H. Martin, Sr.
Reverend Willa C. Martin
Reverend Dr. Victoria W. M. Martin Phd, Phd

To each and every one of my planet earth family members.

I love each of you with all my heart

SpiritMan

Testimonials

SpiritMan's fantastic poetry made me stand up and take notice of the powerful beauty within his transformational Spoken Words. SpiritMan is a Master Poet. His vocal renditions are miraculous and inspiring to hear. — Victor Love-Philosopher X, CEO/Author/Speaker, Menwomenfixit.com

*****

Whenever I hear or read a SpiritMan poem, I smile and say to myself, "Ain't that the truth." His words are a beacon of light shining on and guiding us toward our better selves. Thank you SpiritMan, I love You Too! — Carole Sallid Times, www. ebizwosmen.com

*****

SpiritMan's poetry speaks to the passion of one's soul. He seeks to satisfy the craving from deep within. Only through such a gift can words wash away all inhibition for life and love through age, wisdom and knowledge. — WC Harris

*****

I love to hear SpiritMan recite poetry. It is so soothing and thought-provoking. He is always a hit with the listeners. Much love to that man of God. — Sylvia Hayes

*****

SpiritMan's poetry is like the voices of heaven with the angels serenading to whoever is listening. I never knew poetry as deep as his and it has caused me to create a new interest in the art of poetry. Thank you SpiritMan for creating a new interest for me. — Cookie Lum

Contents

Dedication	i
Testimonials	ii
Chapter 1	1
Love	2
Unedited – Uncensored – Uninhibited	3
Soul Mate / Soulmate	4
Forever	5
Inspiration	6
Silence is Golden	7
The Time Is Now	8
The Very Last Day	11
A Dream	12
The Canary	13
Thought / Energy	15
Chapter 2	16
A'on is Bett'n Na'on	17
Attention, Thoughts and Feelings	18
Stand Your Ground	20
Intention	21
Competition	22
Code of Silence	23
Critical Change	25
Is it true?	27

If	29
Coat and Hat	30
You	31
Love, Love, Love	33
Chapter 3	35
The Eternal Quest	36
The Grand Harmony	38
Consecration	40
Invocation	41
The Lord's Prayer	42
Philanthropy	43
Magician / Trickster	44
The Same Old B. S.	45
Starting Point	47
Simplicity / Logic	49
Wishes	50
Forgiveness	52
Chapter 4	54
Religion	55
Angels	57
The Rainbow	59
The Rain	61
Prayer	63
Awakening	65
Dedication	66

Information	67
The Master	68
Nature	70
Night Time Sky	72
Deliberate Thought	74
Chapter 5	76
Creator	77
Rescue	79
Patience	80
Wipe the Mirror	82
Fear	84
Right Reverend Church	85
The Absolute	88
Trees	89
The Open Flame	90
Am I Awake, Am I Asleep, Is This A Dream	92
Intelligence	95
Chapter 6	97
The Bird in the Bush	98
Manly P Hall	100
Authority	102
Presence	104
Improbability	106
Overview	107
The Way	109

Questions 110
Demonstration 112
Impatience 113
Results 115
Negativity 117
Chapter 7 119
   I Am God 120
   Alive Alive Alive 121
   Light vs Shadow 123
   Associations 125
   Thought Focus 126
   Consciousness 128
   The Tunnel 130
   Keepers of the Light 132
   The Echo 135
   Existence 137
   Boundaries 138
   Believing / Perceiving 139
Chapter 8 140
   Limitations 141
   Profane / Profound 142
   Stagnation 143
   The Procession 144
   Family 147
   Be God 149

Un - Do	152
Prediction	154
I Am Only Human	156
Ethics / Morality / Integrity	158
Words	160
The Message	162
Chapter 9	164
The Center	165
On A Rainy Day	167
Silhouette / Icon	168
Me	170
Commitment	172
One	173
One Mind	175
Brilliance	176
External	178
Dash	179
The Universal Language	181
About the Author	183

Chapter 1

Love

Love gives life to vibration
Love gives form to things
Love is the breath of the heart
Love causes everything

A most powerful, powerful energy
Through the ages has passed the test of time
Penetrating, emanating, pulsating, palpitating
Love supremely sublime

Many tall romantic orders quite often go unfulfilled
Too much asking, too much tasking, too much force of will
Not knowing what to do, say or think when all goes so very well
Trembling, fearful, tearful, so very hard to tell

First lines of defense are clearly broken through
So exact, so complete, what will you say, what will you do
Are you too strong, brave and powerful to succumb to the primal call
Long before, much too powerful to ignore, love will make you fall

Unedited – Uncensored – Uninhibited

Unedited, uncensored, uninhibited you say
Bashful, quiet, not talking today
Looking and listening just to feel what I feel
Questions looming, mind zooming, is what I feel real

Feelings within me wanting so to be free
I dare not reveal these feelings so deep inside of me
I'm tossing, and I am turning, not knowing what to do
Dare not display it, yet I want to say it to you

It is embarrassingly honest and painfully abrupt
I catch myself thinking thoughts, God, surely, I should interrupt
As I observe, looking and searching for just one clue
Amazingly I find all my thoughts are of you

You are more important to me than I have ever said
Can't hold this inside me, no more room inside my head
My heart too is filled, doing everything it can do
Synergy, strong energy, I must share this with you

You are everything, you are everything to me
You are not a fantasy, you are not a dream, you are my reality
More honest, more truthful, more alive and more real
Unedited, uncensored, uninhibited, is how you make me feel

Soul Mate / Soulmate

Soul Mate or Soulmate is it one word or two
What do you believe when you think it through
The concept is about blending, two souls into one
Activity begins between two friends, perhaps it's all in fun

Spirits interweave, intentions undisclosed
Feelings once hidden, now revealingly exposed
Quite capable of shielding all my woes and all my fears
Playing no games, my emotions are tamed, what have we here

I've been known to self-talk, in a kind of therapy if you will
Where once there was emptiness, thru this therapy seems to be filled
Something's happened, it feels now that it's not only me
I ask myself, is there someone else, or just what could this possibly be

I have never ever been lonely, I can spend time with myself
I can be very good company even if there is no one else
What once satisfied me, no longer my hunger feeds
It seems that I am only one part, of my soul felt needs

How could this have happened to me, I'm tested, tried and true
Thoughts I focused on myself, I find them all dwelling on you
I no longer feel complete, I feel so isolated and so alone
You complete my soul, you dispel the cold, like warmth,
where the sun has shone

Forever

Do you believe in forever
Is forever really, really true
Is forever what dreams are made of
Nothing to hold on too

Yes, I do believe in forever
Tomorrow is my rule of thumb
Yes, and I too have heard it said
Tomorrow will never ever come

By thinking thoughts about tomorrow
While contemplating what I'll do
Since tomorrow will never, ever come
I will spend forever and ever loving you

Inspiration

Inspiration comes from so very deep within
Deep rumbles and groans to the surface ascend
Music, messages, images, passions, released from its clutch
Infrequently, rarely, if ever, most often never, ever touched

Inspiration summons a response to a specific call
Oblivious to most and surely not understood by all
On certain special occasions, when timing is exactly right
Inspiration surfaces revealing hidden pleasures and treasures to the light

Upon first revelation what's revealed might not be known
A limited view, to whom it's due, to the one who stands alone
Something beckons from so very far, far away
For seconds, for minutes, for lifetimes, perhaps for just one day

Inspiration wells up from so very deep within
It comes with quiet, soft spoken refrain
If you focus more closely and listen attentively
Inspiration just may whisper your name

The Universal Language

Silence is Golden

It is often said that silence is golden
Reading between spaces and lines
To the one whom pays close attention
Who really knows what, one will find

What is the universal vibration
A language understood by one and all
Only the Fluent in the language of the silence
Can discern the silent call

The deep, deep penetrating silence
Oh, so very loud that all can hear
But only few, is one on them you
Who will choose to draw near

There are those who fear the silence
Perhaps they are just afraid of fear
However, if you are afraid to listen
There is nothing, no-thing, for you to hear

Now if you are one of the fearless
And your heart is true, and your heart is sincere
Listen to the voice of the silence
As it whispers wisdom in your ear

The Time Is Now

The time is now, the time has come
We must now take full responsibility for each and everyone
There is a collective frequency that is contributed to by all
It is the only barometer by which we rise or by which we fall

We are at the threshold of a new transitional age
Yes, it is time for us to turn to an unwritten page
Everything for all to see is in plain unobstructed view
The writing on the very next page can only be written by me and you

We are the next page responsible come what will, come what may
It is written by how we think, what we do and not by what we say
Old messages and practices will no longer suffice
Giving, helping, sharing, caring and loving is my advice

It's time for the alignment, an impending galactic shift
We determine evolution, revolution, or a cataclysmic rift
Promotion of fear is not intended, but you must understand what I mean
If we mix yellow with blue, we are absolutely certain to get green

A frequency is simply a vibration, based on an exact irrefutable law
Unseen emissaries can only come and report what they saw
Our GMO productivity was clearly projected, we didn't intend red, we meant green
Unrecoverable, irreversible barren devastated scenes

The Universal Language

Hunger, homelessness, sickness, destitution can never ever go away
By exhausting, technological and financial resources in war games everyday
How long will it take us to realize that we are all sisters and brothers
There is no one else to fight, no one else to kill, unless we kill and fight each other

The only way that we can ever possibly keep ourselves alive
The collective frequency must show us fit to live and approve us worthy to survive
We search the cosmos looking to communicate with others we believe to be far way
You tell me, would you befriend women and men who fight and kill each other everyday

Is this so hard to understand, it can be understood quite easily
All we need to understand is, without wisdom we cannot escape catastrophe
You ask me, SpiritMan what can I do, I am only one among many
E pluribus unum, I will share with you the exponential game of doubling the penny.

The compound dynamics of multiplication is a fascinating fact
We played this game as children, you remember so now let's bring the game back
I will give you just one penny. I want you to double it everyday
One penny, two pennies, four pennies, eight, continue on in this same way

When you get to day ten you will have one thousand and twenty-four
On day twenty you will have a considerable amount more
Now take your calculator and continue to play this binary number game
What you will find in a very short time are numbers that are impossible to contain.

SpiritMan

If this could happen with one penny, now think of people as one
The exponential factor works oh so quickly and soon our work is done
Each one, reach one, it's just that simple, that is all we have to do
The universe has given us this simple strategy now it's up to me and up to you

Time is not running out this is the evolution of human existence
Past advanced civilizations vanished perhaps due to their resistance
Social, ecological, economic meltdown or will we break through
The time is now, the decision can only be made by me and you

This is the final answer with the sustainable clearly in our view
Our survival is a matter of conscious, deliberate choice,
future determined right now by what we do
Love is the final answer, yes, Love all by itself
Love is all that will save us, unless there is no love left

The Universal Language

The Very Last Day

If today were my very last day, what would you say to me
Would we maintain status quo, or is there some impending need for an apology
Spoken words are sometimes invalid, what you do is what you really mean
Should we patiently, quietly wait and observe passing scenes

After the fact sometimes too vivid, because of things we might have said
Intentions are so much better expressed, instead of trapped inside our heads
If I could just recapture this fleeting, foregone opportunity
I could think of many things to say you, and things I hope you'd say to me

Foreknowing is a refined sense, as in precognition if you will
Between the known and the unknown there are many spaces to be filled
This could be the last time I have this chance and this opportunity to say
Exactly what I'd want you to know on this my very last day

I don't want my last utterances to be lost in memory
No clever quips, quotes or quirks to define or detail my history
I simply want you to know, that I love you
And I will love you again and again and again
Distance, space, time, nor death can conquer love, nothing can

A Dream

Is a dream a waking reality, is a waking reality a dream
Do you always mean what you say, do you always say what you mean
Are your thoughts different from your reality,
are your words different from what they express
Is the thinker separate from the thought, is the thinker more or is the thinker less

Let me ask you about an illusion, something different from your reality
Like a desert mirage, far too large to be what and where it appears to be
That's because it is all in your head, like a dream instead, like a fleeting fantasy
I ask myself, what could this be because it seems so very real to me

Too much invested in appearances and not enough in that which is real
Only upon awakening, found to be nothing more than just a passing thrill
A passing thrill can appear fulfilling; a passing thrill can almost seem alive
That's only due to, too much dynamic energy, yet it's all mentally contrived

I have been called a dreamer, in some whimsical, fanciful sense
Dreams are the fabric of an evolving reality, expressed in the future perfect tense
There is an energy projectile that penetrates the unknown
Only dreams fit this description, as light reveals the un-shown

You can never separate the dream from the dreamer,
nor the dreamer, from the dream
This is a duality, reality, expressed as the scene and the un-scene
You will never find dreams without dreamers, for in fact there are actually none
In order for the dream and or the dreamer to exist, they can only co-exist as one

The Canary

Sitting on a perch in a coal mine, awaiting a final fate
Making absolutely certain the observers know, that it is not too late
Someone must always be watching, otherwise the observer will never know
That time might have already come and expired in which we can all safely go

What is a canary sitting on a perch, in some allegorical sense
Is everything swell, is it going so well, is it fabricated, or is it pretense
There are many, many canaries, sentinels and oracles that be
Who is watching the perch, who will be the very first to see

Are bees canaries among other species extinct
Silently attest to the observer, like secrets being held by the sphinx
When will we pay attention, while there still may be time
In which to recover from practices with consequences that are yet undefined

Is the observer the keeper of some secret
Will the observer tell us what to do
Can I get the answers I need from the observer
Can I get a straight answer from you

Do trees qualify as canaries, sitting silently on a perch
Excessive deforestation rampant everywhere on mother earth
Does the observer know one of the things that recycles the very air that we breathe
Do you know that one of those things might quite possibly be the trees

SpiritMan

Earthquakes, hurricanes, tornados, wildfires, mudslides for day and days
Does the frequency of turbulence, suggest we might consider changing our ways
Sperm count, human male considerably less than men a hundred years ago
Does this qualify man as a canary or is this something you'd rather not know

The canary gives its life so that the observer will know what to do
A word to the wise for us to remain alive the only observer is you
Oh and the other observer is me but before I'm done,
 just one more pun, there is No Plan B

The Universal Language

Thought / Energy

Energy in, energy out, is the exact same energy
The difference is how energy is used, determines what the energy will be
Thought create the forms that give energy particles, space to occupy
When your plans don't materialize do you ever stop and wonder why

The only directive for energy, is your capacity for thought
Dissipated energy, incessant thinking are all mental battles that are ill-fought
We all have the ability to control and influence external events
Without consciously directed thought, it's represented as unexpressed intent

As we evolve in consciousness and impose the will to do have and to be
Much to our surprise, right before our very eyes, we create our own reality
Knowing that you are a creator, is the true and proper perspective
Therefore, it is encumbered upon you to be very thought selective

There are those who know this is right, there are others who believe it is wrong
Pay attention to your thoughts and feelings, you won't have to study long
Bad thoughts and feelings cannot create good ones this is a fact in actuality
Don't be misled, be encouraged instead, your thoughts shape and create your reality

Monitor your thoughts and your feelings, it is most essential that you do
Change bad thoughts and bad feelings for good ones, this will work well for you
Go into your heart and into your memory and remember a time when you felt good
You ask, should I do this when I feel bad, the answer is unequivocally, yes you should

Chapter 2

The Universal Language

A'on is Bett'n Na'on
(Something is better than Nothing)

Do you express gratitude for all of the things that you possess
Are you grateful for having more, or do you see what you have as less
Do you say because, I don't have it right now, it is most likely that I won't
If I am grateful will my desires appear as in poof, or am I to blame if they don't

Be careful with your thoughts and feelings and with the words you choose to say
Examine and pay close attention, be mindful each and every single day.
It doesn't matter if you have everything or if you are just getting by
The only thing that really matters is if you are grateful as you try.

There will always be aspirations and something to be achieved
The driving catalyst is anchored in what you really, and truly believe
Avoid negative verbal expressions, what you say may not be meant
Nevertheless, though said in jest, it too must go where onto it is sent

In reality you have everything that life and love has to offer
You are the keeper and the possessor of the keys to all of life's coffers
Where all that you could ever have is contained right here within
Gratitude must precede all thought and continue until fruitions end

In old down-home vernacular, my mother phrased it best
She said it is not so very important if you have more or if you have less
All things begin in the invisible, long before they are seen
A'on is Bett'n Na'on, the fatted calf is much better than the lean

SpiritMan

Attention, Thoughts and Feelings

Some things kept from us as secrets, are perhaps best not known
There are some things left undisturbed that might be best left alone
However, this very moment is a fact in your living reality
It is everything you perceive, taste, touch, hear, smell and see

Too much contemplating the future, no time for right now
Real time in this moment participation is the only way to know how
Many aspire to be masters, but you cannot be someone else
Best master of all, too few answer the call, is to be master of yourself

Can you control your breath and your thoughts, can you control how you feel
Are you blown here and there, like tall blades of grass in a field
Thinking thoughts anticipating tomorrow, no thought invested in today
When the time comes for you to follow through, what will you have to say

Knowing comes by way of repetition, to be practiced again and again
Many practice steps must be taken before becoming the best that you can
This makes the journey engaging and it can sometimes be described as fun
When you think you are being tried and tested, remember the task that you're on.

There is a corresponding balance that compensates for the pendulum swing
All adversity and all elation are quite the opposite thing
You must remain in the balance, equally positioned between the two
Whichever of the opposites present themselves you will know exactly what to do.

Be calm, be patient, be quiet and understand just one thing
No matter what the situation, its' opposite too it will bring
Don't be alarmed looking, searching and seeking answers here and there
It doesn't matter for what you are seeking they all exist as a pair

The Universal Language

So depending on how you are feeling and what your feelings have to tell
You determine upon which of the opposites you allow your attention to dwell
Your attention is a magnet that it attracts energy unto itself
Pay attention to your attention if you want to attract something else

The soil has no knowledge whatsoever of the seed type or seed kind
It only knows the law that bears the grapes of the kindred wine
So never expect fruit from an unlikely or from an opposite seed
Your attention, thoughts and feelings are upon which all creation feeds

SpiritMan

Stand Your Ground

The place upon which you stand is important as a matter of fact
Even though the place sometimes feels under unseen attack
Don't bother seeking shelter, where there is no shelter to be found
Your most empowering measure of protection is to stand your ground

When retreat mode is considered, it is necessary to turn your back
This posture invites the inevitability of a rear attack
When you face your opposition, no matter how formidable opposition seems
Opposition hesitates, halts and wonders if the end truly justifies the means

Sometimes split-second hesitation is the only advantage to be found
This advantage only presents itself when you stand your ground
Fear can be most debilitating, frozen in space frozen in time
Under fear infused conditions resourcefulness is difficult to find

When you need to respond appropriately look within don't look around
Your most appropriate response will only come when you stand your ground
Standing you ground in not about winning or losing or about how you can fight
Standing you ground is not about strength or power or who is wrong or wright

Standing your ground is about representing, when there is no one else
You will be called to give it your all, then you will represent yourself
In the final analysis, it's not important who lost or who won
Champions can't and don't win by forfeiture; the battle is undisputed when done

With hands raised high, with that look in your eye
As you slowly and carefully look around
Everywhere that you go the whole world will know
That you will stand your ground

Intention

Intention is deliberate, intention is intended to be
Intention takes place deep, deep within the heart of me.
I do it because I mean it, I do it because it is true
Intention is purely something you intend to do

There are times when somethings might not be intended
These are times when results might need be amended
It is impossible for intention to deliberately self-misrepresent
Intention can only reflect upon that for which is truly meant

Quite often we ask the question, what is this occasion
Intention rarely if ever needs any explanation
Whether visible or invisible intention is always known
It represents evidence like a blade of steel well honed

If at any point in time, intention reveals the unexpected
This might quite well be a point in time when deception is detected
Intention aligns itself, just like the magnetic poles
Intention is the only true language if the truth be told

Competition

To live by and thrive on competition, no room for creativity
This assures you will not always win, this is your guarantee
Change is an eternal constant, results not always the same
No matter how hard we try, change is certain to remain

Can I force my way of thinking, do I expect you to agree
Am I always considered right, will you always agree with me
There are those who force agendas, will this rule always be
There will come a time, rules are set by others than the powers that be

Outsourcing, bidding wars, no competition please
No tariffs, no taxes, no licensing, no fees
Outsourced employment, production and manufacture
To continue this way, our way of life, is soon to fracture

We rely on our leaders to lead us each and everyday
But it seems that it always turns out the exact same way
It is time to take action concerning the way we are to go
One percent controlling everything, it is time to say no

Do you like how you are living, do you feel in control
Do you think it is better to be passive, or is it better to be bold
You can make a difference; it is time for change
Competitions reign is over, things will no longer remain the same

The Universal Language

Code of Silence

Silence is a time-tested tradition, based on everything you achieve
Quietude is not merely a suggestion, nor does it matter if you believe
This is a message only for those who have ears to hear
This is the place to create that which you hold near and dear

All creation is projected from within the silence, with no sound being made
Dissipation and exertion of energy is where consequences are weighed
Do you really want what you say that you want or is this just idle chatter
Are you really, truly interested in learning to convert energy into matter

Mind is the only converter that can convert energy into physical form
Idle chatter disintegrates matter, now you have been informed
There is no requirement to be a master; you just need to be masterful
Quietly focus on the code of silence, for there in will you find the jewel

The jewel of which I speak is the jewel of creativity
Hold fast be true to the task, the results you will certainly see
This is an important knowledge, in fact it is imperative that you know
This will keep you from faltering, with energies blown hither and fro

Practice does not promise perfection, nor the best of the best
Its only guarantee is if you practice, you will progress
Progression is forward movement that moves progressively ahead
Empowered by concentrated focus yet embellished by the unsaid

Remember the code of silence for this is the creator's tool
This is the unshakable foundation where those who create rule
You are in fact a natural, for the secret science of the silent code
Before you came into existence, the silence was your abode

Never ever forget the silence, from within it are all things projected
Energy unformed, before it is born, this is how it must be protected
I have shared with you a vital secret, practiced only by a select few
I suspect, you are ready to project, I leave the code of silence with you

The Universal Language

Critical Change

Critical change is when and where we effect the vital change
This is the critical point where things can no longer remain the same
There are many things that are constant, however, change is not on this list
Unless you list change as a constant, only at this place can change exist

Making a change can be formidable, if you make the change by force
Pushing, shoving, jockeying for position, pressing to establish your course
It is all but impossible for you to force the inevitability of change
Metamorphosis, what kind of force it this, nothing remains the same

There are certain rites of passage that take place naturally
Tap into it, and you will experience your eventuality
Becoming involves anticipation and sometimes elation too
Let go, you will be the first to know, when the change comes over you

Critical change guarantees that change is definitely certain
So gradual, so fragile, you will know when you have parted the curtain
Stepping through is a major event upon every individual's horizon
Critical change is a knowing, nothing to look for or keep your eyes on

There is no need to spend time casting your gaze afar
This change is a becoming it is actually who and what you are
As change takes place in the butterfly, so will it take place in you
You will soar forever more when your critical change comes through

SpiritMan

Not possible to avert or to delay this critical change
You are fully aware, nothing can or will remain the same
When it is time for the baby chick, to break the confinement of the shell
You don't have to wait, never too late, natural instincts always tell

Confinement, constriction, panic, impossible for you to breathe
This is natural for the critical change to be conceived
Rise up and acknowledge, for your critical change is here
Prepare to soar, there is so much more, you have nothing to fear

Is it true?

It is true there is a creator of each and everything
Is it true that in my hands I hold the controlling reigns
Is it true that I am actually the one who is in control
Is it true that it's all up to me, if the truth be told.

Is it as true as truth could ever, ever be
Is it true that there is an awesome power alive inside of me
Is it true that this can and should be easily understood
Is it true if anyone is to believe this I surely should

Is it true, through this power I can do anything
Is it true to this power all cares and concerns I will bring
It is true that in this power, I live, I move and be
Is it true that this power is the only reality

Is it true in the acorn is found where the mighty oaks grow
Is it true that everything is within that I really need to know
Is it true that all knowledge is found at the hearts center
Is it true that this is the only place that I need to truly enter

Is it true the image and the likeness of the oak is in the acorn seed
Is it true in the acorns heart is everything that the mighty oak needs
Is it true that all growing and becoming can only take place within
Is it true that this is the place my plans, passions and purposes begin

SpiritMan

Is it true that there is an image and likeness alive inside of me
Is it true or is this just some passing glimpse of eccentricity
Is it true that all I will ever need I had right from the start
Is it true that all I will require is securely held within my heart

Is it true that the same intelligence in the acorn exist in me
Is it true that this is where I will find special gifts, talents and abilities
Is it true that this knowledge will actually work well for you
Enter your heart from the very start, you will perceive what to do

The Universal Language

If

If I called the shots and made all the rules
If someone sells something at any price they choose
If price too exorbitant, don't bother to ask why
If it's too expensive can't afford it, no need to try

If consumption consumes, what happens when there is nothing left
If after everything is gone will consumption consume itself
If we continue these practices in which we engage everyday
If we refuse to change, will consumption ever go away

If we send all our jobs and money to places far away
If we can't thrive on promises made from day to day
If no one is paying attention, no one is mining the store
If we don't take control soon there will be nothing more

If we assume that all is well and soon we will recover
If we think little of ourselves and much less of one another
If we leave everything to fate, to caprice and to happen stance
If we don't stop now, soon we won't have a ghost of a chance.

What if?

SpiritMan

Coat and Hat

Coat and hat signify coming and or going, as in a metaphor
Remain still before you move, know exactly what the movement is for
Is your movement for a specific purpose or do you just want to go
Is this a question for which you have no answer or is your answer, I don't know

Just wanting to go can be called restless, so sit and rest a while.
Lay back with energy intact, take your shoes off country style.
In order to be masterful, you must compel the body to obey
The body must always do what you want, the body must always do as you say.

There are many coat and hat wanderers moving here and moving there
Hooked on sensation hooked on stimulation, you can see them everywhere
When you sit and embrace the stillness, you derive powers unexpressed
The choice is yours, to plot your course north, south, east or west.

When next you take up your coat and hat, know the direction in which you will go
Be aware of the reason and the direction, it is very important that you know
If your coat and hat are not essential, perhaps where you are might be best
Breathe, be still, be silent, be calm, these are attributes that masters possess.

You

Looking for you is an understatement
My search was far and wide
The reason I have stopped searching
For I have found you here inside

My heart beats only for you
This it will always continue to do
You feel what I feel; we know that it's real
Because you feel the same way too

Our search is now over
There is no need to fear
Blended rays of the sun, hearts beat as one
You know that I am here

When the anticipated event arises
You will know that it is me
No requirement for spoken words
We use the silent frequency

Words give flight to thoughts
As birds are lifted on wings
The wind is the breath of loves song
Thoughts of love makes our hearts sing

SpiritMan

I am not in an all frenzied hurry
I know that you are here
I wait patiently to breathe upon you
I will wait for you, I will persevere

Does waiting make the heart grow fonder
No work here for waiting to do
As a matter of fact, waiting is under attack
For I am already here for you

I know that waiting can make you tired
I too feel the same fatigue
Wait a little longer as love grows stronger
We only think of it as intrigue

You already have me
You know where I am from
I am right here waiting within you
I am your chosen one

Our communication is very specific
A language no one else can detect
We speak with our eyes and with our hearts
Only with us, will this message connect

The Universal Language

Love, Love, Love

Love is life's most cherished possession,
It's much more than something to do.
No need to take heed on itself does it feed
It goes out and it comes back to you.

It flows powerfully through you
So very natural so it seems
In its naturally evolving passage
No need for excesses or extremes.

Love needs no object of its attention,
It inundates and flows universally
No need to qualify or make mention.
It grows fully exposed infinitesimally

Love travels everywhere
It travels to places unknown
It just flows, where ever love goes
Love will never leave you alone.

You are a vessel, of loves ebb and flow
Powerful primal energy all will come to know
A natural synergy, powerful magnetic energy
Its radiance felt everywhere you go.

Share love everywhere, wherever you are
For the love that you share is your guiding star
Love has power, love knows no deceit
The love that you share is the only love you keep

Love can't be contained, you cannot harness what is free
When not being shared love is simply dormant energy
Energy in waiting so apparent, not all can see
Loves fate, opens the hearts gate, it flows effortlessly

Love is something that you cannot see
Though unseen, you are certain of its' reality
Pay love attention, it is impossible to resist
You are loves only vessel and only through you, can love exist

Love makes no one more special, than anyone else
Knowing this, is where you will find your true self
Love flows through everyone at all points in time
Tune in and only then loves frequency you will find

Feeling less than loving, having less than loving thoughts
If loves energy does not flow, loving lessons can't be taught
Love is calibrated to the frequency of the magnetic love law
Very alive yet can't survive if no love energy upon which to draw

Chapter 3

SpiritMan

The Eternal Quest

The unanswered questions of Aristotle, Plato and Socrates
Answers sought by them, may I have the answer please
Who and where is God and why am I here
Is there a reason or do I remain beset by fear

Many questions and answers seemingly held in trust
Tell me who holds the secret, of who created us
knowledge of most things, somewhat limited knowledge of that
Why do these answers evade us, what are the actual facts

Always asking the question, is there someone else
Are we here all alone, or am I all by myself
Will we ever find the real answers that we need
Continuing to create that upon which to inquiringly feed

Perhaps these are not the questions to ask
Maybe just questions that fuel an unknown task
Earth, air, fire and water, things that cause us to be
Time to know the truth of our living reality

This energy that creates everything including you and me
Play of electrons, cosmic symphony, blended in perfect harmony
Harmony is the basic reason, the reason why and who we are
No need, for a distant case to plead, by casting attention afar

The Universal Language

There are questions, with answers, `we do not know
Attention projected outwardly is where attention will go
We have pondered the far reaches of space and galactic time
The questions are still unanswered, what do we hope to find

What is the highest number, or the dimension of hyper-space
Intellectual contortions, mental calisthenics starring us in the face
As every infant is born, yes and everyone will die,
Don't stress over dying, daily living is your reason why

I am not the keeper of the secret, I do have something to share
A secret is a secret, because it is not known everywhere
The secret of the eternal quest is accessible to one and to all
As we look up calling skyward, inwardly is where to direct our call

The Grand Harmony

As each and every one comes into existence
Someone is here to guide and to show the way
At your transition, someone will be there for you
Don't waste energy anticipating that day

Don't fret over big bangs, or over the age of the ageless
In this present moment is where your time is invested best
I know you want answers, this for some will always be
Not for all at every point in time, this is an evolving eternity

There are precise answers, as to why you are here
We have nothing to be afraid of and no-thing to fear
There is a revelation for you as to why, where and who is God
No complexity here, you will not find this to be hard

We are here to integrate into the grand harmony
Perfect order and predictable sequences, are here for all to see
All are players in the cosmic orchestra, many players, comprise the throng
There is but one grand harmony, to this harmony we all belong

When we blend into the grand harmony everything self reveals
Perceived in everything we discern and in everything that we feel
We are here to evolve into the very best human beings we can be
When its time to move on, we move on quite naturally.

The Universal Language

Is there really a God, who listens, who observes and who knows
Order, exactitude, time and space in such intricate patterns flows
Is this random, accidental, incidental or some explosive event
Is it consciously evolving hyper-genius of the highest cosmic intent

The grand harmony is not an experiment, nor is it accidental
It is mathematics that transcend measurement, cosmologically transcendental
A conscious expression of perfection that is continually self-revealing
Realization makes us fully aware, with what we are dealing

Stars, planets, galaxies, enumerable universes, throughout the grand harmony
How long, how far, how many, how is this relevant to me
Our task and our commission is to serve every human need
Everyone on planet earth must integrate into the grand harmony

Our duties and responsibilities as human beings must be done
No rapture, salvation, no evacuation, for we are the chosen ones
We are the saviors for each and every individual human soul
This is the reason why we exist, now that the truth has been told

Now, you are fully aware of this most powerful secret
You now know the real truth of the grand harmony
You have already passed every basic human test
Now be the very best human being you can be

Consecration

Presence in all that is, and over all that will ever be
Transmitting loving thoughts to everyone I see
Forgotten are errors of the past, until this present time
No generational curses or original sins of any kind

The misguided actions, reactions, infraction and violations of law
Fathers and children were freed by the light of truth they saw
All is corrected through love, correct thinking, and pure intention
No Guilt, no remorse, no shame, no need of which to make mention

Image and likeness is the result of eternal and unconditional love
Emanating, radiating, reciprocating from within, below and above
Source of the seen the unseen, source of all things manifested
I am a whole-hearted expression of love, tried, proven and tested

I am free of errant thought patterns, impure actions, and desires
I am pure spirit, I am spiritually aware, I am what spirit requires
Evolving in spirit understanding and spirit knowledge as well
The message of light and love is the only message spirit has to tell

I am health, I am abundance, I am happiness, I am fulfillment
I am a student of spirit; my thoughts cause realities existence
All that pertains to me is purged through and by way of spirit
This is the message to all who have the discerning ear to hear it

I discern through spirit presence, this presence inside of me
I am wisdom, power and dominion, over patterns of energy
This power comes from the source, the source found deep within
This power accomplishes everything that spirit lovingly intends

Invocation

Light, love, oneness, thought word and deed
I project image and likeness as creative energy
It shapes my life, creates my results and causes my reality
It is the cause aligned with the laws of all that pertains to me

Natural energy directive of thoughts, feelings, and desire
All pervading unconditional love constructs all to which I aspire
The harmony of energy, wisdom and understanding of natural law
The materialization of energy particles is what the laws are for

I am freedom of expression, spirit expresses freely through me
It causes fulfillment, it causes wellbeing, it causes every possibility
With the speed of thought I direct universal and unconditional love
It emanates from the eternal source within not from above

I announce this invocation through, thought, love and the spoken word
This is an important message among other messages you have heard
Spirit presence, spirit power, spirit consciousness, spirit reality
Live, move, and have your being fully expressed in and as me

The Lord's Prayer

Eternal Source who art within me, exalted is thy name
Thy kingdom come, my kingdom come are one in the same
Thy will be done in heaven and earth as it is done in me
Thy will is expressed throughout all existence, universally

I receive this day and every day, complete and total sustenance
I am free of debt and I release others regardless of the substance
I am led by light and love this is my eternal reality
Reflecting all that I am, thy image and likeness for all to see

I am delivered from all perceptions of love-less-ness
No errant patterns of energy, anywhere to be found
Ours is the kingdom, the power, and the glory
No impure intentions, only light and love abound

The Universal Language

Philanthropy

Philanthropy is love for human kind
How possible is it philanthropic love to find
Every man and every woman for him or herself
No time, for love to find, no time for anyone else

It saddens me to see so much needless suffering and pain
I often ask why is it from this we don't refrain
This cannot be intentional, nor can it continue to be
Soon a time, will appear in our minds, that ends suffering and poverty

Seeing others suffering so badly
Could it possibly be that we don't care
Not hard to find poverty and suffering
You can see it everywhere

We certainly have more than enough
No more tough gets going when the going gets rough
More than enough for you, more than enough for me
We can eradicate all vestiges of suffering and poverty

Human suffering, the stench of a diseased cell
Before too long, the entire organism begins to smell
Continuing to ignore the failure, of cell by cell by cell
By ignoring individual signs soon the whole body will fail

This can be averted by those of us who know
Enough for one and all is the direction in which we are to go
If we want to know the truth, the truth is plain to see
This is the true meaning of love for human kind and of philanthropy

SpiritMan

Magician / Trickster

What really takes place with abracadabra
Is it true, or is it something I am actually after
Short cuts in magic, slight of hand and such
Do I believe, am I naïve, am I in the magicians clutch

I am sensible, I am logical and yes, I am smart
Playing with emotions, led to believe that it's the heart
All in the mind, feelings and emotions are after the fact
With feelings and emotions, logic comes under attack

Step back and gather all your sensitivities
Not taking time to gather, your senses may take leave
Taking leave of the senses, nothing more to be said
No activity, no mobility, it's all taking place in the head

Say to one who is psychotic, no one is really there
Psychotic looks to find the psychotic in your stare
Watch the magician, watch the hands also watch the eyes
Through misdirection, you can easily be caught by surprise

Surprised by the magician, belief in that which is not
Blank stare, no speech, no emotions, no feelings, no thought
When you suspect abracadabra, look into the magician's eyes
You are now redirecting, and the magician gets caught by surprise

The Same Old B. S.

A limited tolerance for BS is what some choose to say
For some reason it escapes me, BS never goes away
Same old BS here, same old BS there
It seems that the same old BS is everywhere

BS has a way of progressively accumulating
You might choose to say BS is proliferating
Nevertheless, there is someone who said it best
Get my boots I'm wading in BS up to my chest

I consider myself among the forward thinking
Difficult to be forward when something starts stinking
Is there no one else bothered, or is it only me
Look around to detect other frowns, mine is all I see

Are we immune to the BS, will it ever go away
Not looking for any remedy just another cliché
Ask someone, how are you doing, not too much to say
It's just the same old BS it's just a different day

This makes one think our tolerance to BS is high
As if to say give me more, I won't bother to ask you why
Relieve myself of this dilemma? I would if I could
If I could relieve the stench, not certain that I should

You see there is a condition called the status quo
Outside of the norm, one should rarely go
The same general consensus, who am I to say no
Tradition says you cannot lead where others refuse to go

BS can be exaggerated nonsense, or boastful talk
To be found wading in BS, you must walk the BS walk
A vulgar expression, has no place in polite society
Must be some space or place, for no BS to be

How much of the BS are you willing to endure
Admitting that this is just more of the same for sure
I want you to know I can really feel your pain
It is time out for the same old BS, it is time for a change

Rid yourself, of this neck deep oozing blight
If it gets any deeper only BS will be in sight
Ridding oneself of BS, too many types to list them
I want you to be rid of your out dated Belief System/BS

Starting Point

When starting out on anything
The most important step is to begin
The beginning marks the start
Until you accomplish the end

It does not matter what the endeavor
All beginnings begin where you are
The desired objective can be near
The desired objective may be far

No one can do this for you
This can only be done by you
Only you can accomplish this objective
Only you can see it through

No one can do your thinking
No one can do your exercise
Mental focus and concentration
Is the only route to the prize

I imagine you want to be fit
Muscular cut and toned
A regimen that must be performed by you
One performed by you alone

If you can do only one push up
Sets of one is what you will have to do
What you will find in a very short time
Your reps will advance to two

Continue this line of progression
No matter, perceived how far
If you maintain you will continually gain
The only place to begin is where you are

This is only a suggestion
But this suggestion will get the job done
This strategy will never fail you
Don't stop before the prize is won

I know this sounds very basic
Basic is how things get done
Do you want to be a master
Masters, master the basics, one by one by one

The Universal Language

Simplicity / Logic

Simplicity and logic represent facility, use, form and style
Simplicity and logic have no need for error or trial
Logic is a basic form of simplicity
Simplicity is that which progresses logically

Technology accomplishes more by expending less
Simplicity is technology at its basic most best
Logic too is technology, with no excessive moving parts
Designed by higher mind, projected from the heart

Simplicity and logic accomplish without excessive push or force
An innate homing signal never veering off course
When we encounter struggling and wrestling everyday
You can be certain this is not the simplest or the most logical way

Simplicity and logic are not short cuts, with just enough to get by
They are the most efficient use of energy, no matter what you try
Simplicity and logic are easy, so it can be easily used by you
Some say it's so easy, that it's too good to be true

You are not here to suffer and to endure insurmountable pain
You are here to learn to magnetically attract, contribute and gain
Simplicity and logic are not some tangible, physical qualities
Product of higher mind, from the beginning of time, the purest realities

The simplest and most logical ways to proceed
The heart and the mind provide all you will need
Remember this lesson, practice it each and every day
Always remember to proceed in the most simple and logical way

SpiritMan

Wishes

Wish, wish, wish say it with me please
Oh, if you would just grant one of these
I would wish for everything that money could buy
Yes, and even the priceless, that too I would try

The word sounds euphoric, smoke filled, dream like
It is spoken like a whisper so very soft, so very light
Sometimes I wonder if wishes really do come true
Do you find yourself feeling and being wishful too

On the other hand, a decision is something you decide
A commanding powerful energy, bold, broad and wide
A decision is what you have decidedly chosen to do
No wish, to establish because all decisions come true

A little secret about wishes and their existence day to day
The least little breeze on one of these just blows them away
A decision is anchored in action and in what you believe
No chance, no circumstance can take what you achieve

I agree, that wishes feel good, this I must admit
Before the wish comes true the creativity goes from it
Wishes honor no commitment, done without a plan
Wish is the bird in the bush and not the bird in the hand

The Universal Language

With decisions you are definitely and truly in control
Wishes are for the whimsical, decisions are for the bold
Confronted with making a decision or the fantasy of a wish
Be bold take control decision should top of your list

Choosing the whimsical, having fun along the way
There will come a time for a decision to save the day
Being in control and knowing is over half of the battle
Instead, the dread of a boat with no engine, no sail or no paddle

Forgiveness

So much talk of forgiveness, will it ever go away
Some things I will not forgive, no matter what you say
Forgiveness is not a matter of choice but an imperative necessity
Its benefit is for the forgiver and not for the forgivee

No such thing as the unforgiveable, there is a different rule
This is a law for the wise, not for those using some different tool
Should you unwisely and foolishly make a deliberate choice not to forgive
You will be very much alive but someone who can never ever live

You are composed of energy, energy that is alive
If this energy cannot flow this energy will be compromised
Compromised energy is another name for stagnation
When you forgive you stop all energy dissipation

Non-forgiveness creates blocked and constricted energy
This energy is the fuel that comprises all reality
Blockage and Constriction retards energies ebb and energies flow
Health, Happiness and Love can't live where energy does not go

Failure to forgive, you commit yourself to a life sentence
Blockage, constriction, failed plans, forgiveness is the repentance
This is not for one who committed some infraction against you
This works for whom the infraction was done too

The Universal Language

Are you considering forgiveness, now that you know the consequences well
Are you emitting forgiving energy, this only you can tell
When you feel un-constricted, when you begin feeling free
You are experiencing free flowing once constricted energy

Your life sentence will be commuted, you will be free
You must remember life requires unblocked free flowing energy
This is perhaps something that you did not know
So forgive, be unblocked, be un-constricted, and you will be free to go.

Chapter 4

The Universal Language

Religion

Does your religion describe how we are to live
Does your religion prescribe what you are to give
Does religion really guide, lead and show you the way
By now we should know most of what your religion has to say.

If I were to teach you about swimming each and everyday
Soon there will be nothing more about swimming left to say
The fact still remains, you've not actually gotten wet
And in all probability, you can't swim, quite yet

How is it that you know all about swimming there is to know
And why is it, that in the water you are still afraid to go
Knowing keeps swimmers up, and non-swimmers down
Most swimmers float, and some non-swimmers drown

Knowing how to swim says one knows that one can float
Not knowing how to swim makes floating remote
Swimmers don't easily go under, they expend effort to go down
Non-swimmers go in, sometimes no swimmer to be found

How is swimming relevant to your religion, anything like being baptized
With a little water on the head and body, a little water in the eyes
Religion is quite a lot like swimming, it cannot be fully taught in class
In the field, is where it's really real and only in the field can the test be passed

SpiritMan

Passing is not verified by testing, nor by quiz, or feat of memory
The intelligence quotient can only be established by what takes place in actuality
Outgrown is the need for classroom lecture and theory as well
The life you live and the service that you give, is the only way to tell

You've surpassed the need for a religious description of the way
The only true meaning of your religion is how you live from day to day
Your religion describes what you should do and what you are to give
The only measure of religion are the ethics, morals and integrities that you live

The Universal Language

Angels

I want to share a secret, perhaps you already know
The secret is angels are found everywhere you go
Angels are assistants who help and guide along the way
Angel's duties are lovingly expressed in action everyday

This is an unknown secret, why hasn't it been leaked
The primary reason is because angels rarely ever speak
Duty is the mark of an angel, not frequently given to speech
This is why so few does this angel distinction reach

Angel action is not determined by angel desire
Oh, and by the way, no celestial angelic choir
As you observe passers-by, much to your surprise
You've looked many angels squarely in the eyes

You cannot recognize angels as they actually appear
No transition, no transformation they are already here
 Where angels are found their duties are quickly done
The way to know about angels is to evolve into one

An angel is not supernatural, they exist quite naturally
Angel transition is not by any means an impossibility
We are aware that this is a vibrating environment
Lovingly raise your vibration with pure loving intent

This is a vital step in progressive human evolution
Angels dispel errant energy patterns, angels cause solutions
You will not visit with an angel to sit and consult
All angel activities are measured in real time results

We think of angels in soft glowing terms of how we feel
Angels are powerful, angels are strong, and angels are real
Angels serve, angels correct, angels are resourceful and brave,
Angels love, Angels protect, angels conquer and save

It is time for your angelic transformation, yes, your time is here
I have shared with you angel wisdom, the angel message is clear
It is important and urgent that this message comes through
The message is human beings are angels, whose angel are you

The Rainbow

Is the rainbow a sign of a promise
Is it a sign of good fortune as well
I will leave the true meaning of the rainbow
For the rainbow observer to tell.

It spans so beautifully across the panoramic sky
When you observe it, do you ever stop and wonder why
Why do rainbows exist, what do rainbows really mean
So vivid, so misty, sometimes barely seen

The rainbow is light, viewed as the individual parts
The parts make the whole, from rainbows end to the rainbows start
Where do rainbows come from, where do rainbows begin
Good fortune is thought to be found at the rainbows end

Spectrum of light, red, yellow, orange, green, purple, violet, blue
Which rainbow color is the favorite color for you
Follow the rainbow, follow it, wherever the rainbow goes
Rainbows final destination no one really knows

Some say a rainbow represents a promise not to destroy
Others follow it in quest and in pursuit of golden joy
Rainbow, the radiance, the brilliance, the energy of the sun
Seven colorful rays of light all blended into one

SpiritMan

Sun in the rainbow as visible vibrating light
Each color individual yet they acquiesce into white
The rainbow is a token of harmony to be observed by all
With promises to keep, or consequences befall

Embracing the earth where the promise was made
A pact to keep, a vow to protect, a duty to save
As keepers we can, and we must prevent a destructive repeat
We must uphold our end of the bargain or from the bargain retreat

There are indications and violations, existing everywhere
We violate the earth, we violate water,
we violate the trees, we violate the air
As keepers of the promise, the promise must surely be kept
If the promise is ever broken there will be no rainbow left

At the rainbows end, no profit, no promise, no purpose,
no pot of gold, no escape plan.
No radiance, no light, no rainbow in a desolate land
What good is a pot gold at the broken promises end
If there is nothing to buy, no one to sell to, and nowhere to spend.

The Rain

From invisible humidity, to mist, to drizzle to drop
From a light sprinkle to a down pour, on every living crop
Crops need not be cultivated to be graced by the rain
They exist to receive the mist, all crops are one in the same

The rain doesn't choose where or upon whom it will shower
Its purpose is to cleanse and to nourish, this is the rains power
To cover, to touch and to give life, to one and to all
This is the reason, and this is the season, for the rain to fall

If you are attentive, you can smell rains announcing breeze
That delicately caresses the earth, the flowers and the trees
It embraces the sense of smell and the other senses can tell
That the rain is ready to fall and to fill every well

A well is any vessel, crevice, cavern or even a creek
The nature of the rain is for its very own level to seek
To make the low places level and the high places low
There are few places on planet earth where the rain does not go

Rain becomes water; it changes to liquid light
Rain goes everywhere, it touches everything in sight
Rain falls so freely, there is nothing we have to do
Naturally abundant, taste it and touch it, as it falls on you

SpiritMan

Just to make mention, a side note to one and to all
Did you know where there are no trees rain rarely falls
This suggests that rain and trees go hand in hand
This is not a message to all creation, just a message to man

Everything is a living part of nature, so too are we
This is a natural paradise, right here is where we are to be
Are you aware that rain and trees have a close connection
Clean and natural solutions are natures only protection

We must move forward in ways for the earth to know
To alternative resources and sustainability we must naturally go
Now is the time for an environmental global strategy
Not comprehending, an unhappy ending to an unnatural tragedy

Prayer

Powerful prayers are silent
Not spoken with the mouth or the mind
This prayer is the prayer of action
Fueled by pure intention is what you'll find

An act expressed through love
In free flowing service to all
This is the most powerful prayer
When you perform this prayer for all

This prayer is specifically for others
This is something some seldom do
It is by far and considerably more powerful
Than the prayers that you pray for you

Prayer is knowledge in motion
You know what you will achieve
Prayer energizes energy particles
Prayer is the result of what you believe

Prayer has gone on for millennia
Asking and pleading on high
The prayer that goes within
Leaves nothing to verify

As we glance into the cosmos
As far as we are able to view
The most powerful prayer destination
Exists within the heart of you

Lines extended outwardly and infinitely directed
When extended you will find no end to be detected
They travel infinitely, yes they travel, without end
This means you are the center, where all things begin

All things evolve from within the center
From the center all creation grows
This is the awareness, this is the wisdom
The one who prays effectively knows

When you choose to pray
Your center is where prayer must go
This is the prayer, this is the time
Upon others loving energy to bestow

Awakening

Belief systems, thoughts, truths, whatever you believe
Frozen frontiers of thought, take your pick from any of these
Expansion of consciousness, the cessation of growth
Committed to the grand scheme by pact or by oath

Zealots attack for not believing, what they believe
One way of living and thinking is what the zealot hopes to achieve
No time for apologies and no place for amends
Failure to comply confronted with an infidels end

You are significant, the universe cannot lie
I too am baffled, please don't ask me why
Appearances disguised as the way things should be
Concerned with how to be seen, yet ignoring what we see

Why am I so concerned about how I appear
Why do I feel so unimportant and so insincere
So important, what I want you to think of me
So much so that I cant see my own reality

Tradition says I am beset by an errant unnatural fear
Control from the days of old, no relief found here
Errant thoughts from antiquity, how much longer will they last
Ignoring progress and pursuing perfection promotes re-living the past

SpiritMan

Dedication

Dedication asks but one thing
What are you really willing to do
If I am willing to share myself
Are you willing to follow through

I will command your undivided attention
I will demand your focus and time
It will most definitely take a while
Before you see results of any kind

I do not give nor offer easily
I do not share with one and all
My orders can be monumental
My orders are engaging and tall

If you will do all that I command
I will place the scepter in your hand
You must make me know and feel
It must be clear your request for me is real

I don't engage in folly, nor do I play games
Only the highest possibilities will I consider or entertain
I know this is difficult, it is possible that you may fail
If you remain loyal, I might allow you to prevail

A revelation not known, but one you must come to know
Your dedication must be obvious, it must actually show
One more component, should you heed dedications call
I share only with the most dedicated, I will not share with all

The Universal Language

Information

When information flows, don't restrict it let it flow
It can only flow to the place where it is intended to go
Information is for the receiver, so pay attention if you will
It is for your desires, thoughts and aspirations to be fulfill

We like to have things go in an even-tempered way
Something to refer to in some practical sequential way
Information is for the purpose, of serving you as you live
A special something to each person, information has to give

You must have something in common with that which you receive
It has everything to do with your thoughts and what you believe
It is very interesting to hear someone say, that I don't believe
They feel this way when not on the same frequency to achieve

Frequencies and feelings operate by exact scientific laws
Unerringly, not directed by the effect, but by the cause
They are designed that way so no mistakes are made
Its' price is for your attention to be fully paid

Information is powerful, too much is not necessary at all
Too much information can overwhelm, rendered unable to recall
One single bit of information, yes all that's needed is one
The correct bit of singular information get's the job done

Be clear with your interest and passions, be certain of your dreams
Interests, aspirations, and passions fuels what your information means
The means by which to orchestrate and to do what you must do
The means, the information and results are all created by you

The Master

Secrets are not only for masters
Secrets are also for you and me
Intended for those who are not masters
To learn to live masterfully

As we aspire to become masters,
We abide by the same rules as do they
At some point in time we hope to find
We too will become masters one day

Until we reach this distinction,
When it is time to become one
Live out each day, the exact same way
As masters before us have done

Anything that you want to do
Practice it as though you already can
You will move closer to your goal
You will begin to more clearly understand

Mistakes are a part of the process
It is not considered failure at all
Mistakes are simply necessary steps
As you march to the Master's call

The Universal Language

See and view mistakes as instructions
That guides you along the way
Soon, soon, very, very soon
There will come that special day

You too will become a master
Master of all that you require
The bonus for your achievement
Is mastery of yourself and all to which you aspire

Nature

I love walking into the forest
Listening to birds near and far
I pick single birds from the sounds
To discover where they are

As each leaf on the trees
Serve as ambient reflective shields
It causes the sound to reverberate
It sounds so vividly surreal

No description for Omni-directionally
Reflected perambulating sound
Only deep inside pristine nature
Is where this experience can be found

There you will find a babbling brook
That adds a chorus to nature's song
Continue and you will see other signs
They reveal themselves as you pass along

You will see mounds built by the ant
Nests constructed by birds
You will see many other life forms
You will listen to and hear their words

You will know, this is a special place
You have entered into nature's heart
Here you will come to know
Of this nature you too are a part

The Universal Language

You are an integral part of nature
Perhaps much to your surprise
You are a very necessary part of it
This you must unequivocally realize

Enter into nature, as often as you can
Upon entering you will fully understand
Separating from nature is unnatural to do
The unnatural is by no means a part of you

The unnatural cannot soothe the spirit
The unnatural cannot caress the soul
The unnatural cannot heal the body
Sensibilities can't unnaturally unfold

As you enter into nature
Experience the freedom found there
It is a wonderful, wonderful place
You will feel it everywhere

Take your time when in nature
Fully feel the energies that be
Look in every possible direction
See all that you can see

You will find it to be a lovely place
One of the loveliest places around
Come back as often as you can
Never forget what you have found

Night Time Sky

No shutter, no blind, no drape, no shade
Night time sky through my bedroom window displayed
From here I closely observe the beautiful night time sky
Sprinkled through the cosmos space and time to defy

The vastness of the universe starring back at me
I enjoy the night time sky seeing all that I can see
I take in constellations, track them across the sky
During my observation a shooting star passes by

This causes me to make a wish as in times before
Past wishes that didn't come true I choose to ignore
Each shooting stars wish, has a life all its own
The wishes from the past are past wishes gone

The night time sky makes one wonder
Exactly why and how things are
Can you answer your own questions
Can the answers be guided by a star

Do you have an inescapable destiny
Prescribed by some cosmic fate
This is light years from what is true
You hold the keys to fates gate

The Universal Language

Believe this because it is actually true
This is the correct consideration for you
Existence is an ongoing evolving occurrence
We seek the fixed and none moving to
guarantee reassurance

The earth is traveling quickly through space and time
The stability that we seek, sometimes hard to find
Though we are in motion, we perceive that we are still
A stabilizing faction of the creators will

This causes the elements to look stable
This makes them appear not to mix
This allows people, places, points in time
Upon which one can become transfixed

Though we are moving so quickly, and we travel so far
The night time sky reveals that we too are a star
Searching the night time sky, with its secrets held in trust
Then the question surfaces, who is looking back at us

Deliberate Thought

Everything necessary is within you
I know that some think it's not
Therein lies the problem
This is simply misdirected thought

In keeping with this line of thinking
Not certain of the way in which to go
As said by "William Shakespeare"
"Thinking makes it so "

Are you deliberately thinking
The thoughts that you want to think
Have your thoughts become too heavy
Are they causing you to sink

If thoughts are unattended they sink into the ground
Adverse conditions, consequences
and circumstances all around
Once you allow them to sink and they sink too low
No thought necessary when up is the only way you can go

You must cultivate a deliberate line of movement
For the energy we describe as thought
You must learn to intentionally direct it
So, no mental battles will have to be fought

The Universal Language

You must begin to move deliberately
Through each day in space and time
Thoughts don't always promote reinvention
Sometimes harmony is what you will find

You will find harmony to be most natural
Inter suspended throughout all that is
The only thing that causes our dilemma
Are deliberate thoughts exchanged for fears

Fear has the capacity to isolate you
Mind frozen in past patterns of thought
It is impossible under these conditions
For free and deliberate thinking to be taught

Chapter 5

The Universal Language

Creator

If I were the creator, what would I create
Would I create evolving expansion or would I create fate
Would I create harmony, would I create love
Would I create conditions that we need to rise above

Would I create borders, would I create war
Would I create enemies, one another to destroy
Would I create sunlight, or smog and toxic mist
Would I create opposition, would I create to co-exist

Would I create careers, would I create passion
Would I create unhappiness, would I create satisfaction
I would be the very best creator that I could
I would create everything a good creator should

We all have an idea of how things should be
Easy to get it right when asked do I want this for me
We are all creators, no one else can get it done
Bring our creative ideas together one by one by one

It is by no means difficult, in fact it's easy to do
All of the creative components will be created by you
Send all soldiers home, confrontation comes to an end
All prisoners educated to reintegrated into society there in

Medication would be free and education too
Freely learn to be and do anything you want to do
You will make contributions, contributions have no cost
Cost levied against education, no contributions is society's lost

All cutting edge technologies will be the rule of thumb
Creating more by expending less, is how this will be done
Profit, greed and consumerism have now had a full run
Antiquated policies and practices, their days are also done

Everything is becoming much better
It is so very plain to see
When we all create together
All will be created by you and by me

Rescue

Adversity unfortunately does in fact exist
In most instances it's quite natural to resist
Resistance however can impede your rescue
Struggling makes it difficult for help to get to you

Like the life guard who goes in for a life to save
Panic stricken, flailing, situation appears grave
To struggle against the life guard is to struggle against rescue
Sometimes necessary for a situation to take hold of you

When you surrender to a situation and stop the push and pull
It then becomes easier to be saved from the drowning pool
Rescue comes from spirit and rescue comes from man
Panic has no boundaries; it is to be as unrestricted as it can

If you continue to fight and struggle, overcome by fear and doubt
It may then become necessary for rescue to knock you out
Rescues will not leave you, because it is far too kind
Rescues standing motto is to leave no one behind

Yes it can be next to impossible for you to clearly see
But there must come a point in time for a glimpse of levity
You are not to struggle and fight against your rescue
Rescues only purpose is that of saving you

Patience

Patience is the art of waiting, the art of waiting patiently
Have faith in the results; anticipate the good of what will be
Waiting has its drawbacks, the calisthenics of the mind
Restlessness, anxiety, anticipation are what you'll find

This is a special time and place to fulfill every desire
Be fully aware that you have everything you require
Faith is knowing, it is the knowledge of what will be
Hold clearly in mind, the visions of your reality

When you invest attention, in fretting over the past
Peering into the future, asking how long will this last
Ignoring the present moment, this moment in which you wait
 This is the moment in which you must fully participate

Waiting makes time appear protracted and long
That is because you are singing the impatient song
We cannot rush that which is truly meant to be
Much like uncovering a seed, to take a look and see

If you uncover the seed, you impede the process of growth
Violated belief in knowing, you have broken the patience oath
Have faith and trust in knowing, the result is soon to come
You are the recipient; yes, you are the chosen one

The Universal Language

Wait patiently; I know you think it's hard to do
Just find that quiet, patient place that is inside of you
Wait there it will not take long, this you will certainly see
What you have expected and waited for so patiently

The result must come, and it will come just for you
Designed with you in mind, you will know what to do
You are to be aware and know the nature of your desire
Just remember to be patient, is all that patience will require

Wipe the Mirror

Wipe the mirror so that you can clearly see
Perhaps not fully obscured, most likely just a little obscurity
Not seeing clearly, not certain of what you see
Might not be certain exactly what the image may be

The mirror can only reflect that which is shown
Anything that is unclear remains part of the unknown
When the mirror is clear and showing exactly what it sees
Clarity always dispels the appearance of fallacies

I looked in the mirror, there I saw a reflection
Just a casual glance, one without close inspection
Then I looked more closely, to see what I could see
I simply and loosely refer to this reflected image as me

Am I what the mirror shows, am I truly there
Is this simply a vibrating play of light, ether and air
I want to see me as I really and truly am
Potential power like waters being held by a dam

A projection is an image that comes from a source
Has the reality and the image ventured off its course
If I don't truly like what I happen to see
I ask myself could this image really be me

The Universal Language

I desire the purest image, reflected from within
Unobstructed light is upon which this image depends
The mirror can only reflect truth, a truth that's plain to see
A truth that is my truth and my purest identity

Who am I really, who really am I
I want to present the purest reflection, don't ask me why
There is something inside me that wants to be the very best
Is this something really me or is it image and likeness

SpiritMan

Fear

Am I uncomfortable with snakes
Because of my mother's fear of worms
Is fear a natural state
Or is it something that one learns

I have heard it said
'Fear is false evidence appearing real"
Whether true or false
Fears, validation is based on how you feel

Infants are born with only two fears
A fear of falling and of a loud noise
All other perceptions of fear
Manipulates feelings and confidence it destroys

Fear only exists, by the way that you feel
By controlling your feelings, you determine what is real
If you are fearless, it is because you have nothing to fear
This is your truth so very plain and clear

When frozen in the moment
Immobilized in space and time
Rendered unable to move
Fear makes solutions impossible to fine

Foot Note: Tony Robbins quote "fear is false evidence appearing real"

Right Reverend Church

Things have not been going well for me
I need to see the Right Reverend Church
I know that my solution is there
The Right Reverend represents God on earth

I know that something is out of order
I know that something is very wrong
I have been going through this situation
For oh so very long

There is something on me
I really need to get it off
I know this is something unnatural
Just how much will it cost

I haven't been to see Right Reverend Church, in quite a while
When I attend, I sit in the same seat on the same aisle
I had to work on Sundays, but I paid my offering and tithes
No body called to check on me, no one even inquired

I know the Right Reverend is very busy
He can't come to see you when you're sick
The Right Reverend is always with you in spirit
To think he is not is one of the devil's tricks

SpiritMan

I really need to go into consultation
To find out what God will have me do
If I invest in the Right Reverend Church
I know God will surely see me through

I cannot really afford private counsel
So, I guess I will just go on inside
As I turned to make my way in
I caught a glimpse of the right reverends ride

This served as my further confirmation
I know that I am in the right place
Only a glimpse was all it took
Windows tinted, couldn't see Right Reverend's face

I know he is Gods' representative
I see all of the visible signs
Coincidently, his ride was a Bentley
What other kind did I expect to find

Upon entering in, I was lead to my familiar seat
Right Reverend Church appeared, all arose to their feet
He said let there be light, and the light was displayed
Heavenly music began, everyone rocked, and everyone swayed

Music so wonderful from the heavenly band
Why do the bodyguards keep the congregation from shaking Right Reverend's hand?
They keep the lovers of the Right Reverend well away
Just close enough to hear what the Right Reverend has to say

The Universal Language

The Right Reverend said todays' lesson is the same as last week
You must remember the earth shall
only be inherited by the weak, oh I meant the meek
Tithes and offerings is the only lesson you must be certain to get
Everyone knows that the Right Reverend goes only by private jet

The Right Reverend said on these solid rocks I stand
The rocks were not on the ground but on the fingers of
Right Reverend and First Lady's hands
There is one thing I want each of you to help me do
There are many mega mansions in my spirit but all I need is two

I listened attentively and very closely to the Right Reverend Church
He looked out and said, would you rob God,
there can be nothing worse
Give me ten percent of your gross and
don't dare let the devil ask you why
When you give your money to me,
you are building your mega mansion in the sky

The Absolute

Knowledge of the absolute, not taught or assimilated in school
This knowledge is revealed by different yet very natural rules
If this was available in the universities and halls of higher learning
Why is it then that for remote places scholar's hearts go yearning

The most learned would certainly this knowledge come to know
Why off the beaten path and to the remote places do they go
The message of the absolute must be quietly discerned from within
Only attained by those who upon this internal journey begin

Life in and of itself is the true meaning of absolute love
By internalizing, the absolute is what we will find the meaning of
Coming to know the absolute, this journey upon which we embark
Some from the intellectual approach, others the approach from the heart

Any approach is acceptable, as long as it leads within
The important aspect of the journey is to quietly begin
When you find that internal space, the space found within
You will travel inwardly, infinitely, the absolute has no end

Trees

Trees represent the life cycle as it was intended to be
It seems that we are removing quite a lot of the trees
We've come through many ages, we know this is wrong
For what reason is it that we deliberately continue on

Soon there will be no reason to express despair
We are embarking upon and entering the age of repair
We are now a cashless society, money nothing more than air
When we cut all of the trees, no more paper money there

We cut trees to make paper money
We make paper money to cut the trees
We cut trees to make brochures
Only to create junk mail out of these

Rest assured this is not how it will continue to be
There are different, alternative measures and possibilities
Trees are a most vital and a very necessary treasure
Vital to the life of one and all, far too vital to measure

We are now embracing the goal of reforestation
The trees are necessary for all future generations
Trees resist the pull gravity, gravity they do defy
They reach onward and upward toward the sky

Trees celebrate the earth, air, water and you and me
Yes, trees recycle the very air that we breathe
Not made to be pieces of paper seeking something to buy
We've outgrown paper printing; lets' give alternatives a try

The Open Flame

The dance, the flicker, the movement of the open flame
So very interesting is it calling my name
I must reach out and touch it, this I have never seen
A magnificent expression of wonder, what does it really mean

I have never seen a sight exactly like this before
For some unknown reason impossible to ignore
I must touch it I want to know how it really feels
I want to know if it's imaginary, I want to know if it's real

There are many open flames, called by other names
In actuality they are really all one in the same
Why can't I resist it, why must I feel its touch
It seems to call to me I want to grasp it in my clutch

Within the desire to know the truth of the open flame
True knowledge of it, comes fully understood as pain
Upon a child's first view, can't resist the open flame
Must reach out to it, must know, what is its' name

Upon reaching, grabbing and holding it, within one's clutch
It immediately reveals I do not want to be touched
Within the first millisecond, the curiosity and the pain
Leaves the indelible memory, this I will not do again

The Universal Language

Never a time of not wanting or desiring to touch some flame
Its nature is to make you look at it, as it calls out your name
When you look around, you can see it in other things
 Sometimes unpleasant, yet necessary is the knowledge it brings

Remorse, regret and knowledge of the open flame
Landmarks in the memory say never pass this way again
Acquisition of this awareness is intense upon its arrival
You will never forget, hardwired to your sense of survival

You may never again be attracted to this particular flame
The lesson is to see it even if it appears by a different name
It is necessary to understand and to know the reason why
Chickens never threatened can never know how to fly

There are times when information can be viewed as a threat
These are reinforcements that make it a lesson you won't forget
Never forget the dancing beguiling call of the open flame
It will always appear, most assuredly by a different name

Am I Awake, Am I Asleep, Is This A Dream

So very calm and peaceful as I lay down to sleep
I lay on my bed and into my head a dream starts to creep
Am I dreaming, am I awake or am I asleep
Thinking and traveling in thought taking a cosmic peek

So serene, I feel like I am floating through the air
moving effortlessly here, moving effortlessly there
As soon as I think or feel it, no matter the place
I recognize scenes as they appear right before my face

Thinking of things that pass as thoughts or so it seems
Am I sleeping am I awake or is this a dream
Beautiful scenes, beautiful places, beautiful people I see
As I think my way toward them I wonder if they can see me

There are faces it seems that I have in some way known
There is also something that feels very much like home
The expressions on the faces are warm and filled with light
I fail to mention, no apprehensions, this feels oh so right

Is this really some place, some place I have known,
It feels so familiar, it feels so much like home
I can go anywhere, I can go anywhere I please
Consciously propelled by thought on a cosmic breeze

The Universal Language

No effort expended, no requirement for physical strength
No attention to distance, duration, space or times length
I can move into places and spaces where ever they are
When visiting them in thought they are never ever far

Am I awake, am I asleep or is this a dream
I feel so very alive, what can this feeling mean
As I travel back to see where the dream began
I travel back through a vaguely familiar land

I travel over housetops I travel through the trees
I Travel effortlessly on a cosmic breeze
I see something, something I remember rather vaguely
It seems that this is a place where I once wanted to be

As I returned to the place where I first fell asleep
I see something I remember as I take a dreamer's peek
I see someone laying in what was once my bed
Am I asleep, am I dreaming, what is this in my head

I come in closer for a more examining view
To my surprise before my eyes, that looks a lot like you
I remember that face, I remember this place,
and I remember everything I see
I look at the face, I feel the feeling is this place,
was that ever really me

SpiritMan

I have no desire to resume, that former familiar space
Too cramped, too crowded, not enough room in this place
Even though it looks so very, very memorable to me
My thoughts reveal the real place I truly want to be

I look at where I came from; I remember where I have been
Not beset with the desire for this old place to re-enter in
I have this freedom, not having known before
Not so aware of time and space, yet aware of so much more

I am now leaving this place, perhaps I will pass this way again
Not saying sooner nor later, not saying exactly when
Am I asleep, Am I awake or is this a dream
I will take my time to discover, what all of this really means

The Universal Language

Intelligence

Why more intellect and less common sense
What is it that fuels our current circumstance
Intelligence is the beneficial use of what you possess
Only from intelligence will anything less digress

Intelligence does not violate the laws of nature
Intelligence does not violate the natural laws of life
Intelligence will not embrace environmental infractions
It will not travel the path that promotes human strife

Choices are very clear, the olive branch or the dove
The concern for all is what intelligence consists of
We have been led to believe, this cannot be done
Intelligence is the place where all conflicts are won

There are courses of action that are beneficial to all
These actions will always answer the universal call
Centuries of conflict and opposition yet no one has won
There is only one winner, when we realize were are all one

Our decisions are those of the elite controlling few
No thought or consideration for what the others will do
There will come a time when all is unmistakably clear
There are actually no others, only you and I are here

We are one family, we are the family of man
We are here to accomplish as much good as we can
There is a natural integrity for the rules of the game
A broken rule or a violated law are one in the same

SpiritMan

Why continue to play a game you can never win
Evidence from times before, yet we don't comprehend
Power, conquering, greed and control will never get results
No more human violations, no more environmental assaults

There is no one else, there is only you and me
This is not at all complicated, it is not difficult to see
With war technologies, you can only destroy yourself
Intelligence cannot serve us, if there is no one left…

Chapter 6

SpiritMan

The Bird in the Bush

The bird in the bush verses the bird in the head
I am sure you have heard all that's been said
Which do I prefer upon closer examination
The bird in the hand or the bird of my imagination

The bird in the bush or the bird in the head
Is much like the handwriting on the wall
Even though it is in plain unobscured view
Yet not clearly understood by all

The bird in the head can be such an elusive sight
When you try to capture it, the bird takes flight
There is a reality, perhaps over rated as well
Reality is what you believe, so your stories tell

Some think reality is composed of considerably more
More than what is in plain view, far too much to ignore
Flowing information, stimulates thoughts and feelings in you
Though clearly visible, can't always see what's in plain view

An alternative choice, a different course of action
Motivated by inquiry, stimulated by distraction
Something different, something totally different to do
Most likely it will not be what's directly in front of you

The Universal Language

Reality is patient, the writing on the wall is succinct
The bird in head or in the bush makes one pause and think
There is a refinement that will naturally in due course align
Its own level, not being resolved and its own reality to find

Not possessing the bird in the bush, you own the bird in the head
Pay attention to your reality and not to the alternatives instead
When entertained by the fanciful and you choose the fantasy
Take your time, with entertainment for the mind,
reality waits patiently

Manly P Hall

(Inspired by Manley P. Hall)

We cannot resist or disregard the natural laws of life
We cannot and should not promote the agenda of human strife
Honesty, integrity, morals, ethics, intelligence, infinite love
No matter what atrocities precede us, we can grow and rise above

Growing the hard way, creates war and environmental violations
There will be poverty, there will be crime, there will be devastations
The compliant way, promotes love, honesty, and education
We will reverence all life, we will honor all creation

Cannot resist the natural law of life to collectively thrive
A significant and graphic difference between thrive and survive
We are to be collectively healthy, collectively safe, and whole
One power, one presence, only one collective soul

Growth will not endorse greed, control, nor the suffering of the masses
It will not perpetuate the proliferation of the few, ignoring life as it passes
The way out of our present difficulty is to realize we are one
Separation, individual agendas, the will of the whole must be done

A house divided, cannot and will not stand
Conquer the selfishness of having others to control and command
There is unity existing within us, it exists most naturally
When not practicing unity, we are practicing futility

The Universal Language

Spiraling uncontrollably and irretrievably out of control
Resulting in infinite chaos nothing of which to take hold
No such thing as failure, no failure in the eternal plan.
Failure is the movement of consequences directed by and toward man

Anything that does not promote life is an adverse possession.
Happiness is natural law, no escape through confession
We are aware of ethics and morals and of integrity
Simply ask yourself would I want this done to me

The only difficulties that exist are those we create.
The advancement of life is in what we must participate.
Domination is the verification of a belief in individuality.
If it does not work for the whole, it is counter productivity

Anything less than the common good, will by law destroy itself.
Self-fighting is suicide, it will consume all that is left.
The life pulse is a single movement toward collective wholeness
Separation, greed, selfishness move toward substantially less

The outworking of the universe is that of order and harmony
No laws for rebellion, irrefutable laws of truth, and unity
The solution is to pay attention to one and to all
By not expressing virtue, by our own vises we will fall

(Some of these lines are from the Manly P. Hall archives.
Rhyme, meter, scheme, and structure by SpiritMan)

Authority

We have been told so many things
Do we really know what is true
So much conjecture, so many opinions
What actually am I to do

Where can I possibly find an authority
To comfort this evolving emptiness of inquiry
Some posture themselves as those who know
Will I know when to the self proclaimed knower I go

Do I seek information, do I seek truth
Will I find what I seek, will it be of any use
Dark sayings rendered in mesmerizing tones
After hearing, I wonder should this be left alone

There are many renderings of mimic and that of parroting
Do the Sayers really know the meanings of the sayings they bring
Are they just saying something, they themselves once were told
Never knowing, never experiencing, never anything to behold

Does the parrot really know what it is saying
Does the parrot only know the desired result
When something is said that someone else said
This means there is no one with whom to consult

The Universal Language

There are knowers who are not actually knowers
Knowing is just something they've learned to say
Not knowing nor imparting wisdom
They simply say it in the exact same way

Does this sound somewhat like a parrot
Does the parrot know what's being said
Don't let just anyone be your authority
Your authority may just be a parrot in your head

Presence

God is all there is, Christ is the conscious awareness of everything
The Whole I Spirit is the facility through which nature is continually creating
I have traveled, and I have worshiped over land and sea
In quest, I must confess a spiritual discovery

I have grown to understand the meaning of the spiritual frequency
Regardless, it does not matter the land, the language, or the geography
I engaged in worship in languages and practices foreign to me
Inter-suspended within the difference was a kindred familiarity

We share different views on ceremony and the names of deity
However, never the less we agree on the one reality
Everything I have come to know has been handed down to me
Accepted or rejected, tuned in on the truth frequency

I grew up attending church, so worship is integrated in me
Each Sunday was predetermined where I would be
I prayed, sang, observed marriages, funerals and baptisms as well
I am fully equipped with church and worship stories to tell

I was so very observant and very inquiring
Observing the emotions expressed by others while spiritually aspiring
These religious experiences are intimate components of me
From the very beginning, no ending to the quest of spiritually

The Universal Language

Thought processes, conclusive and non-conclusive findings
Questioning, investigating, inquisitive, toward what am I inclining
I didn't seem to feel or receive the spiritual animation
What's wrong, why don't I shout or have some religious exclamation

My inquires became more penetrating to study spiritual law
Buddhism, Islam, Metaphysics, Mysticism, are different aspects that I saw
I studied science of mind to discover the laws governing thought
Quietly I found that too much thinking also places one at fault

As a result I have an innate awareness of God and Existence
God is All and All is God is the reality that dispels resistance
The more one tries to disqualify the reality or the concept of God
It becomes increasingly more impossible to shatter oneness into parts

Improbability

If I had a bucket of black ink
I would look into it and start to think
Cardboard, paper, glue, and thread
Improbable thoughts begin to enter my head

I would mix together all of the components
I would shake it up and dash it to the floor
Haphazardly an encyclopedia appears
A result like this, who could ignore

When we observe physical existence
There is awe and wonder in every direction
Season, cycles, nature, the grand cosmos
All one harmonious expression

The science, the mathematics, the accuracies
Attest to logic, order, intricacy and Predictabilities
No random, no haphazard sequences or anomalies
Perfect order and exactitude is a fact in all of these

Could everything be accidental or incidental
Is it without intelligent directive
This would and could only mean
We are not of this evidence receptive

The facts and the findings are before you.
You have valid and substantiated proof
Is your position, one asserting the intelligent directive
Or did everything just appear, as in poooffff.

Overview

Scientific, spiritual, philosophical overview
Shedding light, seeking answers, wanting to know what is true
From an individual perspective my personal assertions find
There is an existing source responsible for everything of every kind

Can you tell me what it is, call it what you will
It permeates all space and time, every energy particle it fills
Yes, even you are immersed in it and composed of it too
This presence is everything and yes it also includes you

Everything everywhere is composed of this single source
The only power, the only energy, the one and only force
You perceive that you are separate and an individual as well
All existence it compels and all fallacies it dispels

There is an awareness referred to as consciousness
An individualized aspect of the source, you are nothing less
Integrated throughout existence, there is only one material
Call it atoms, call it energy, call it primal, call it ethereal

There are those who question the intelligence of being
Investigate by asking eye witnesses, what are they seeing
Leaves fall in autumn, salmon return to their original home
Everything is in perfect order; does it function on its own

There are so many variables, some moving and some fixed
Yet so orderly, so perfect, future times and dates one predicts
It is quite alright to continue with this existence overview
You will find no inconsistences when the overview is through

The inquiring toddler, learning to talk, every question ends in why
Can't answer the toddlers every question, but you can always try
What is the highest number, what are the dimensions of the sky
Order, exactitude, precision, will a non-intelligent origin, defy

The Way

The way is by no means a direction, the way is the way to live
Pure intentions, love and dedication, you must be willing to give
Service is also a component of how to express from day to day
Awareness, light, and compassion will be cultivated along the way

Manifestation will begin to show itself, detachment will also pay
Non-criticism and singleness of purpose to be offered everyday
Non-obstruction and pure motives will create your every success
This will insure that life is expressed at its fullest and its' best

To achieve you must be constant and impersonal as well
The way harbors some secrets, yet is has so much to tell
Thought purification is an imperative, you must always feel good
When you live the way, the way will be clearly understood

Questions

Do you believe in a higher power
Do you believe there is a God
Do you believe there is power in prayer
Or is it all just a façade

Is there really anyone listening
Anyone really listening when I pray
My personal choice to hear my own voice
Just to listen to what I have to say

Do prayers really get answered
Is there a devil, what part does he play
Does God allow the devil to test your faith
Just to see if your faith will go away

Tell me is there any such thing as magic
Was Jesus actually deity too
Is heaven real, or is it what I want to feel
When my time here on earth is through

Will I ever really live again
Is there more to life, or is this it
Why do I question all that I have been told
Why don't all the pieces seem to fit

The Universal Language

Is there a looming generational curse
How does it equate to what's in my purse
A price to pay, some mystical words to say
Is this the only way, I can avoid the worst

Why can't I find love, why does love avoid me
Am I looking in wrong places for loves face to see
Will I find my purpose, the true meaning to why I exist
You will eventually correctly answer every question on this list

Demonstration

To demonstrate you must know your result
This is for you, no need for others to consult
Be still physically, this aspect is essential
Be quiet and still to arrive at the maximum potential

Relax control nerve impulses and muscles too
This is required for your demonstration to come through
See the final result as you would see it in a vision
Let go and release, to demonstrate with accurate precision

Anger, hatred, guilt, envy, sorrow, remorse
Disappointment and not forgiving takes you far off course
You must forgive yourself for all that you have done
There is no other forgiver, you are the forgiving one

You too must forgive others for the wrongs they have done
After forgiving them, all forgiveness battles are won
At this point your demonstration is not hard to see
Here is where from old appearances you break free

Remain clear and focused on your central idea
You are now in the realm of the demonstration sphere
Your thoughts will wonder from time to time
Bring them back into alignment with higher mind

With practice you will with all energies align
Meditating for frequent short periods of time
This is the key and soon you will begin to see
Manifesting, attracting and demonstrating your reality

Impatience

In a society of instant gratification
Having it now is the new norm
With short cuts and immediate results
Nature was obviously not informed

We are an integral part of nature
Immersed in the natural scheme of things
Though we have a desire for instant gratification
All creation not intended to have wings

We create stress of the highest magnitude
When we can't have it now
Pushing and pressing takes us out of the creative
The instantaneous keeps one from knowing how

Forcing it right now, creates an awkward position
This is your guarantee of some real opposition
I'm not saying don't try, because all hope is lost
An investment of time is actually, the only cost

I am naturally optimistic, most all of the time
When out of sequence, the un-natural is what you find
No matter how instantly things may and do appear
A systematic progression can also be found here

In nature despite how quickly things take place
The speed of the planets moving at a blinding pace
There are quick advances, there is the naturally slow
As in seasons, cultivating abilities and watching children grow

Anything of depth, of dimension and of quality
Requires an imperative sequence in time
Virtuosity and highly developed skills
Are some results only time can refine

Results

How you interpret life is how life responds
Beliefs, instincts and experiences is how the fabric is spun
The conscious, the subconscious, the unique mind
From within this dynamic do our realities unwind

Does the universe love me, do I love myself
Without self-love, no love anywhere else
The sentient energy that responds and returns to me
Is the exact replication of my transmitted frequency

My body, my feelings, my mind, my patterns of perception
Seeing, hearing, tasting, touching, smelling, senses reception
Interpreted sense data, distinguishes one thing from the other
Perceptions not absolute, understood differently by another

Conditioned, perceptions, body sickening
Mindfulness is being aware of thoughts quickening
Concentration is the focus of thought, undistracted
The integrity of the results that are being attracted

An objective must be started, and you must continue
When you cling you suffer, you must flow freely into
Right effort, right mindfulness, right concentration
No greed, no hatred, no delusion, no hesitation

Aspire toward the pleasant and the unpleasant avert
Liberation is impossible when on constant alert
Natural clarity of mind is clouded by delusion
Observing wholesome moments, finds the solution

Always consider right efforts, know what you are aiming for
While treading the path, know the path is also what you are
The silence along the way is your ability to be undistracted
Naturally, selflessly your aspirations are being attracted

(Thoughts inspired by Bruce Lipton)

Negativity

How do you prepare to become successful
Are there any negative conditions in your mind
If negative conditions invade your thoughts
Their way to the surface they will find

If negatives are internal, they are external as well
These conditions, makes your future easy to foretell
Life is the point where spirit and substance converge
You are the portal, through which all things emerge

It is necessary for all resistance to be released
Otherwise can't realize the spirit substance feast
Observe every situation that has caused you pain
Be mindful not to cause other's energies to drain

You must name every situation in this process
They are intimate to you, so you can do this best
Do not act or react out of wounded-ness
This way the results will be to that which you can attest

Negative situations determine how you react
They also definitely determine how you feel
Acting or reacting from a place where you are hurting
Makes the negatives appear to be more real

Wounded-ness can't have a different response
Wounded-ness leaves memories of how it was once
Forgive others and be forgiven by those who forgive you
Not enough just to say I forgive, forgive is what you must do

You are learning to act through spirit alone
Spirit impulse creates the results all on its own
The one outstanding fact is that spirit is pure
Through spirit, considerably fewer negatives to endure

Spirit can't be compromised nor can anything else
Conditions can't change if you compromise yourself
It does not matter if you pray or how much you affirm
By embodying negativity, positive lessons can't be learned

Chapter 7

SpiritMan

I Am God

I am not a bearded male who sits in heaven on high
When prayers go unanswered do you ever wonder why
Do you know what you are saying to whom, are you praying
Unanswered results misunderstood, it seems you are playing

You cannot think that I am here, and you are there
Making claims supported by nothing other than thin air
You think I want to punish you, you think I want you to suffer
Can't come to me unless you go through some other

I can only speak to you in the language of truth
If you don't practice truth, for you truth will have no use
Much like inputting all the right numbers, in wrong sequence
Numbers incorrect impossible to connect, wrong residence

So, you speak to me in ways you were told to do
The way to speak to me is the way I speak to you
In order to understand, the language must be the same
Speak to me in the language of truth and from all others refrain

You do not have to seek me, no need to look far and wide
I am where I have always been, right here inside
Needless to look outward and upward, can't on sight depend
I will never ever leave you, I will always live within

The Universal Language

Alive Alive Alive

Is alive just living or is living just being alive
Is living just living or are we just trying to survive
Is surviving living or is it just being alive
Do we live while we are alive, do we thrive when we survive

A play on life and living and an additional play on words
Survival is not really playing as most of us have heard
Struggles contrived for the living, to simply to stay alive
To get through this day, I do what I need to do to survive

There is an additional awareness one might consider other wise
The concept is not a concept about or on how to survive
It is not about struggle, is not about just keeping alive
This concept is about expansion and how we are to thrive

You must consider the difference contain herein
Your point of view is upon which your outcome depends
Do you want to live so you can barely survive
Tell me do you want to be one who thrives

Do you know what is required, for you to survive
Do you know the components of how to remain alive
Just as you are aware of the foregoing in this wise
You must also so be aware of what's required to thrive

SpiritMan

Thriving among other things is very intimate to you
Knowledge of exactly what is required for you to do
Be aware at all times the direction thriving must go
Thriving cannot be vague it must your passions show

Initially write it so you will know what thriving entails
You are the central character of which the thriving story tells
Write it, know it, and look at it through out each day
Carry it on your person, carry it in your heart,
this is the thriver's way

If you are not intimately familiar and aware of your thriving
Not recognizing it when you see it is simply surviving
It will only appear as a stranger, as do other passers by
No idea of the thriving message, not knowing what to try

It is intended for you to thrive, this is natural to all life
That which does not serve, only contributes to your strife
Strife is by no means striving, they are quite different in fact
To be fully alive, you must thrive, anything less is a broken pact

The Universal Language

Light vs Shadow

Light is everywhere present, and it travels instantly
Where there is no light present, darkness is all you see
The absence of light can control you, it can control how you feel
Darkness and shadow can cause fear, but fear is not actually real

Light never has to struggle with shadows or darkness
They occupy difference spaces at different times
When you seek what causes the shadows and the darkness
Blockage and obstruction of light is what you will find

Of what are you really and truly fearful
Is it the blockage or is it how you feel
When you begin to feel better
Know that shadows and darkness are not real

Light versus shadows and darkness
Must observe which way you are facing
When your back is turned to the light
Perhaps your steps require retracing

You cast a shadow, when you are not facing the light
Among other shadows, your own shadow can induce fright
Are you contributing to the thing which causes you to fear
So afraid is the game fear plays, so what have we here

SpiritMan

Just remember fear is nothing more than a feeling
You can determine exactly how you want to feel
Remember this and you must never ever forget
That shadows and darkness are not actually real

So now you ask what is the remedy
How can I possibly overcome fear and fright
You will always overcome darkness and shadow
If you remember to keep facing the light

The Universal Language

Associations

Are you living freely, are you squandering time
Is your life simple, is it complex, tell me, what you find
We create our own complications, perhaps not intentionally
Placing the blame by asking who could have done this to me

Association is significantly important in personal development
Pay attention to associations, avoid unwelcome consequence
Association is like an electronic radio frequency
It hones in on the associated signal quite accurately

It is the same with any signal or any particular habit
Association creates a pattern, before you know it, you have it
When you focus in on any given particular endeavor
Association is better when your acquaintances are cleaver

Someone who represents exactly what you want to do or be
This association shows what you want and need to see
No need to find a master, no need for a guru
Mirror someone who's doing exactly what you want to do

Sometimes, frustrated, exhausted and stressed out
A beneficial time for a mentor without a doubt
Look for flashes of momentum, breakthroughs and success
This happens when associations are the very best

Only balanced harmonious frequencies can or will blend
Feel for the harmonious balance of the company you are in
Only harmonious associations are to be placed on your list
They are easily recognizable, they are impossible to miss

SpiritMan

Thought Focus

When constantly thinking, thought takes on life all its' own
Looming thoughts of helplessness, makes one feel very alone
Like a song trapped in your head, as it continues to repeat
How did it get there, so difficult to bare, how can I find relief

Don't feel bad, all have habitual patterns of thought
To change or to eradicate, this battle constantly fought
Fortunately for you, the first step has already been taken
First be aware, this is how these thoughts get shaken

This is the only point where you can possibly begin
You must be aware of the condition, your thoughts are in
Changing focus by giant steps, you take unnecessary chances
Thru mini steps, this is how thoughtlessness advances

The unique thing about this process is that you cannot get it wrong
Slowly move toward thoughtlessness, leave incessant thinking alone
There is a perfect order, where rampant thinking will be solved
This level is where excessive thoughts, actually get dissolved

Thought is your spiritual nature, you access thought most naturally
You are as much a component of nature, as the earth, air, and sea
Anything that you want to accomplish, it must be taken in
Not pieces too large to ingest, bite size is what nature recommends

The Universal Language

Becoming immediately thoughtless, is too big a step to take
First step in thoughtlessness, is to find a quiet place
Sit and take in a long slow and naturally filling breath
Slowly exhale, listen to your heart and allow nature to do the rest

Your heart is your personal cadence to the universe and to life
Thinking will become less, as being severed by natures knife
Listen to your heart for one minute and then listen for two
Increase the time, continue to listen as fewer thoughts come to you

Surprisingly you might be astounded, at what else you might hear
The more you become quict and listen, fewer thoughts will interfere
This is how to receive messages from the higher sphere
Thoughts will be replaced by messages that are crystal clear

Consciousness

Internal and external awareness, consciousness says it best
Of what are we actually conscious, to what can we attest
Piercing the vail of awareness to glean a look within
Our state of consciousness is upon what our knowing depends

The difference between consciousness and knowing
Are they one in the same
Consciousness is knowing, knowing is consciousness
Are they just called by a different name

Do you think there are levels of consciousness
And what do levels actually mean
Is a level of consciousness, tangible or intangible
Can a level of consciousness be seen

I have heard that consciousness can be high
I have also heard that it can be low
Upon which elevation are you participating
Could is be that you don't really know

Consciousness is represented as feeling
Not necessarily a place that you go
It is an internal awareness of who you are
To be conscious is a feeling that you know

The Universal Language

Knowing is the refining quality
As in being consciously aware
It is the accumulation of everything,
Consciousness penetrates everything, everywhere

There is no ending to consciousness
There is no ending to all you can know
There is no way to rush it or force it
There is no particular place you must go

Conscious awareness exists within you
It exists fully right where you are
It progresses sequentially and naturally
The next progression in consciousness, is never far

SpiritMan

The Tunnel

Moving through life, living from day to day
People and places as I pass along the way
Not seeing anything different, from times before
Surprisingly, a tunnel appears, without a door

I walk into the tunnel, I felt compelled to go there
Light was fading, darkness shading, triple blackness, thick air
Guided by hands and fingers touching the tunnel wall
No sight, no light, the triple darkness, the tunnel was all

Walking ever so cautiously, placing each step reservedly
Why am I here, what am I doing, what has come over me.
Ordinarily I'd have no desire for this tunnel to enter in
It feels eerily familiar, like some place I might have been

Darkness ever so confining, no hands before my face
A redefined darkness, it consumed time and space
Thinking of my location and what possibly would I find
Passing thoughts, skirting the periphery of my mind

Darkness all encompassing, no thought of anything else
It absorbed distance, space, time, location and myself
Don't know how far I have come, I have no point of reference
Can't define space or time, no placement no preference

I have come much too far to turn back now
Disorienting, no tunnel ending, turn back, don't know how
Not fearing or feeling any cause for alarm
I move slowly onward never thinking of being harmed

The Universal Language

I hear a faint sound, what could that be in this place
Moving ever closer, I see a mirror reflection of my face
I move closer to the advancing mirror I see
Oh, it is not a mirror, another person looking just like me

Forehead to forehead, nose to nose, and chin to chin
I ask this identical person tell me where have you been
I have been where you have been, I know all you have known
Yes, your most intimate secrets, when you thought you were alone

I did everything you did, until the deed was done
Today is the day that we come to know that we are one
We establish so many acquaintances, with everyone else
The most important acquaintance of all is the one with myself

As I passed thru my double, as my double passes thru me
Everything is the same, again triple blackness is all I see
Without making a sound, without saying a word
I can hear my double thinking, I understood all I heard

From this very day forward and throughout all eternity
I understand clearly what I do to you I actually do to me
This not only applies to me, but also to everyone else
The only person you can ever hurt is none other than myself

As you proceed thru your tunnel, be mindful of all you do
You do nothing to anyone else, you can only do it to you
So be willing to accept the consequence of everything you do
No regrets, if you never forget, what you do, you do to you

SpiritMan

Keepers of the Light

There are those who promote darkness
No conception of that which is right
They promote a one-sided agenda
No consideration for keeping the light

The only light of which they are aware
Are the rays of the sun and the movement of air
There is a light of which they think much less
The illuminating light of consciousness

Making a concerted effort to keep others down
Living in opulence beyond any other opulence to be found
Doing all that can be done to cause suffering and misery
Answers quite clear if asked, would I want this for me

Payment given to institutions of higher learning
To promote blind agendas without administrations discerning
Why and for what possible reasons are they paying
What are students learning, what are the professors saying

Pollution of the environment and the pollution of the mind
Deliberately obscuring the light, what do they hope to find
Violating all the rules that apply to human decency
No concern for how it affects others, just what's in it for me

The Universal Language

Pressing, promoting, and pushing hopelessness as the way
Hope, the masses dope, craving it, every single day
Making certain, only the few have peace of mind
Nothing better to do, so the few choose to be unkind

Actions thought to be void of balancing consequence
Enforcement, no time spent, nothing relevant, no need for defense
Only major players can and are allowed to play this game
The results in every instance, all turns out the same

People are dying, families are crying, all is fair in love and war
Power brokers lying, no attempt at trying, nothing to answer for
There is a light, and this light we all must share
Without this light the shadow of darkness is cast everywhere

Come to journeys end, time on earth is done
I conquered every foe, every battle, I have won
A corollary, a balancing result of the light
For the promoters of darkness, no light, no sight

Who can fix this, what on earth can I do
Answer comes to mind, must be corrected by you
Please forgive my mistake, this darkness I cannot take
This cannot be my fate, I beg you, for heavens sake

No one to direct prayer to, nothing you can do
Single handedly and deliberately, orchestrated by you
The darkness is not eternal, it will eventually go away
Maybe years, centuries or eons, most certainly not today

SpiritMan

The balancing corollary compensates, for everything we do
Just remember every consequence is constructed by you
Groping in self-imposed darkness, day after day after day
Status large, fully in charge, only time makes darkness go away

How long is this hopeless, blinding darkness
How long is this disorienting absence of sight
The requirement is to go long and distant into the darkness
As is required to become a keeper of the light

The Echo

Standing on a mountain precipice
Facing an unsurmountable wall
Vibrating, undulating, perambulating
Shouting a powerful call

Saying it only one time
Yet it repeats again and again
Impacting resounding compounding
Echoing as often as it can

When I say what I say
Does the echo know what I mean
Why does it repeat over and over
Can its purpose be clearly seen

By not paying attention
By not heeding the echo's call
The result of the echo
will potentially affect us all

The vibrating echo energy
Does not have a single clue
Despite at what conclusion you arrive
It takes its directive from you

If things are not how you want them
Do they have a life of their own
When saying things you don't mean
idle statements should be left alone

When words go out unattended
Saying whatever comes to mind
Unaware and you haven't a care
Don't be surprised by what you find

Words repeated over and over
Respond as hypnotic prayer
faced with the result no one to consult
Not an option who gives a care

Remember the rule of the echo
It can only do what you say
Your life is an echo expression
Of what you intone and speak everyday

Existence

What is the meaning of existence
Do we live only to subsist
Subsistence is just enough to get by
What kind of existence is this

Would you believe if I told you
You are entitled to everything you desire
Yes, I do mean everything
Everything that you could possibly require

We exist to amply fulfill our every need
Wants wishes hopes dreams desires yes all of these
Appearing differently, we choose not to believe
Thinking makes it so in everything you achieve

A key component of existence
All must most assuredly learn
Everything that concerns you
Must be for the good of all concerned

We exist to unfold our every possible passion
Everything is here, every shape form and fashion
Existence only exists to be of service you
Express your purest passions,
existence must follow thru

Boundaries

Boundaries that limit the body
Boundaries that confound the mind
Boundaries seen and unseen
Boundaries of every kind

Self-imposed limiting boundaries
Boundaries of mores and folkways too
Boundaries that you mistakenly find
Boundaries that unfortunately find you

Boundaries can be sometimes invisible
Yet they too can be so very real
There are physical boundaries you can see
There are some boundaries you can only feel

Boundaries are not the rules
Boundaries just tend to get in the way
Boundaries cannot stop you
They compel you to invent another way

Invention is not aware of any boundaries
New rules are created as you go
Boundaries tend to be stationary
Boundlessness is what boundaries
will never ever know

Believing / Perceiving

Reality, perception do you believe what you perceive
Is reality what you perceive or is it what you believe
If you are going forward if you are backing in
The reality and the perception are upon which you depend

It is perhaps not as though it might appear
Believing says it is and perception says it's here
Vibration pulsation throbbing in my brain
Perception and belief not always the same

Moving through space, evolving through time
Belief or perception, truth is what I seek to find
Is this something that is received by force of will
It is that which allows truth to naturally be fulfilled

Not always certain about that which I perceive
Over shadowed by the thoughts of what I believe
Perception and belief are aspects of a different kind
Perceiving and believing are components of a single mind

Chapter 8

Limitations

Are limitation imposed
Your guess is as good as mine
Is it that to which one is exposed
What does one expect to find

When limited in thought and action
What is one to do
Limitation is practiced
Not something imposed on you

Some break free of limitation
it is called freedom of choice
Will you allow limitation to prevail
will you be an outspoken voice

Profane / Profound

We have equal access to the characters twenty-six
Do we create the profound or upon the profane transfixed
No one does your choosing, you choose what you express
Profound or profane your choice made without duress

Graphic expletives that reflect and allude to gender
N word, B word, F word , which do you choose to render
Being insensitive and just saying whatever you want to say
How would you feel if presented to you in the same way

There are innumerable sensitivities, there is one for you
When targeted by the profane, exactly what is one to do
Would you become irate or would you be profane as well
Would you be influenced, would the effect be easy to tell

The twenty-six characters are equally accessed by you and me
Will you choose the profound or will you choose profanity
The words that you say and the sounds that you make
Ripple effects universal energy much like and earth quake

Will you contribute to the stability of the profound
Will you allow profanity to continue to abound
The profane destabilizes cosmic, global energy
The profound contributes to universal harmony

By happen stance or by deliberate choice
By whatever measure or persuasion you choose
Despite what you think as life's camera shutter blinks
You determine if the profound or the profane you use

Stagnation

When things tend to appear stagnant
Not being quite certain of what to do
Thinking, thinking, thinking, and thinking
Yet you haven't got a clue

When you seek a potential solution
One thing you must remember to do
Remain with the tried and tested
For it will see you through

There may appear to be times and places
Where nothing seems to move
You might be sensitive to a positive feeling
You may feel you are about to lose

Gestation is quiet, and it is silent as well
Sometimes movement, is difficult to tell
Place your attention on the hour hand of the clock
You can't see if moving although it never ever stops

So, in looking and seeking solutions
Where there appear to be none
Remain with the tried and tested
And follow through is how it's done

SpiritMan

The Procession

Standing in the procession
That has existed from the advent of time
Places faces steps and traces
Impressions in the sands of time

We never know our position
We never know when our number is called
Assuredly we know that the procession
In most instances is the same for all

We hear that familiars have made it
They have come to the procession's end
The quality of one's advancing procession
Solely on that individual depends

No matter how or what you may feel
No matter what you are compelled to do
The procession will be experienced by everyone
All will proceed, all will follow through

When will my time come to go
When will I step from the processions line
How will I know the coming next phase
How will I recognize the next phase in time

There is ample time for preparation
Do I have time to make a procession plan
Am I to wait, how do I participate
Can I make my procession exit on demand

The Universal Language

No need for foreboding
No reason to impose undue strife
You only need to be aware
Processions end is the continuation of life

Why be afraid to speculate
Do you really want to know
When your time will come
That from the procession you will go

In this eternal grand procession
Spaces places sequences for one and all
Listen and pay quiet attention
To the cadence of the processions call

You know that you will make it
Because each and every one will
Thinking wondering and contemplating
Exactly how do you really, really feel

Sometimes there comes a sadness
Hearing someone stepped out of the line
You are incorrect in feeling sadness
We will all have our special time

There is an elaborate celebration
In some cases, quiet lamentations
There are rituals and ceremonies as well
A final intoning of the ending bell

SpiritMan

Not possible to know who is next in line
Can't see the beginning or the end
Knowing where you are right now
Is all upon which you must depend

Go to various places look into different faces
Ask what in heavens name am I to do
The procession is not quite the same for all
The answers you seek are here inside of you

There are many who have gone on before
There are many who have yet to come
Are they all different individual existences
Might they just all possibly be one

One energy one substance one consciousness
Perceived individuality separates us from the rest
I can see you and you can see me
Nothing more than an illusion of individuality

The procession is an eternal perception in time
Memories of experiences of past procession lines
Will the procession change, will it go away
The procession is eternal, today is procession day

Family

Who actually is our family
What things do we need to understand
It is simply a message of oneness
All are members of the family of man

Quite true that we have different appearances
We are of every color tone and hue
Every human being on planet earth
Is directly related to you

Family composed of many members
Some members you seldomly see
 regular and everyday members
Ones you see infrequently

There is this kindred connection
A connection that comes from with in
 every human being on planet earth
Is your very next of kin

Taking things into consideration
The message rings load and clear
Family not defined by the geographical
Such as who is far and who is very near

Family is that which allows us to hear
To hear the familiar connecting call
The one kindred living consciousness
That flows through one and all

If you are not certain of family
I will make it very, very clear
This message you must clearly understand
This message we all must hear

Here are the various relationships
The ones of which family is meant to be
When you look into someone's eyes
Just know this one is related to me

The entire world consists of mothers and fathers
Those older by a generation in age
Brother and sisters are those we find
Right here on the same page

Sons and daughters are a generation younger
The ones we teach and lead
They are the ones in our declining years
That we will most assuredly need

One relationship remaining
Significant other or a best friend
This can be and evolving energy
Evolving into committed next of kin

There are many moving components
There are various essential parts
The only thing that holds family together
Is a love shared from heart to heart

Be God

Imagining is somewhat like pretending
Children don't find this very hard
While we are imagining and pretending
Let's just pretend that we are God

You have made mention of image and likeness
Exactly what did you really mean
Was it just rhetoric or banter in passing
Just a line in an unscripted scene

Imagination is a necessary part of acting
So that you fully engage the part
Acting out the total role of the character
This role must come from your heart

Live, think and breathe every part of your role
This is a spirit filled character prompted by your soul
No miss ques or blunders you will know everything to do
This is the act of creation and the central character is you

The more you study, embody, and rehearse your part
You will notice that you are actually becoming God
You will begin to live move and be as God would be
The temple of the living God is the purest form of deity

Though I say that I am pretending is this really so
Convincingly undeniably my godliness begins to show
As I continue to imagine I choose to tell no one else
So, I say as I contemplate one day I believe this myself

SpiritMan

The confirmation for this new way that I feel
Sick ones that I think of lovingly begin to heal
Paying no attention to the appearance is not very hard
Now I look on everything lovingly and I see it as God

Persisting in the new way and relinquishing the old
An act of God is energy projected from my soul
The ability to correct to protect and to perfect
This newly found attribute of my God aspect

The old way creeps in to take a final shot
It says who do you think you are surely God you are not
Some may call it blasphemy to say that I am God
You choose to win or lose you also choose your part

Some actors create command performances
There are others who support behind the scenes
Will this character be your ongoing reality
Will you pretend that it's only a dream

Every pretense is an act of believing
Fully believing is knowing as well
Believing and knowing is the converging point
Where your godliness begins to excel

As you look upon appearances
See them as God would have them be
You will start to shape a new landscape
On the whole of all reality

The Universal Language

A child pretends to be a doctor
Another pretends to be a movie star
You begin to no longer defend
No need to pretend who and what you are

As you embrace this new realization
Effortlessly, naturally no old paths to trod
I am the only hearer as I look into the mirror
I am image and likeness, and the living presence of God

Un - Do

How can I un eat it
How can I un say it
How can I un do it
How can I make it go away

I don't want to feel guilty
Somethings I wish I could un say
Various events at points in time
I just wish they could go away

There are some certain things
Some experience you cant un-know
There are places that you have traveled
You wish that you could un-go

Somethings remain, come what will or may
Redirected thinking can make them go away
Sometimes unaware of my choices ripple effect
Only after the fact do I these ripples detect

There is no place for guilt regret or remorse
Only the absolute result of a previous choice
Through vigilant desire to rectify the way
focus only on the things that you want to stay

If by chance past thoughts should ever come back
Make them fully aware that they are still under attack
Don't harbor, think of, or embellish them in thought
Somethings to be dismissed, not battles to be fought

The Universal Language

Like a breath of wind blows the leaves away
What you will un do is done in the very same way
Bearing in mind things that are not actually good
I want them to go away I really wish they would

Redirect thoughts putting desires in their place
In time un-dos will no longer appear before you face
At this point in time you will be able to say
Now is the time and today is my day

No more struggles with misplaced ongoing attempts
Free from pre-existing un-dos I am now exempt
Do what you say and mean what you do
Bearing this in mind there will be nothing to un-do

Prediction

Prediction announces that which is yet to be
Not knowing, yet showing, what's ahead of me
Make it, influence it, effect causality
I solely create what lies ahead of me

Prediction is foreknowing, it bespeaks a certain fate
An adventure in which you alone participate
Not imposing mindless banter as you go along
In quietude, the more powerful, the more strong

I am free to suggest and free to disclose
Not freely to others plans exposed
To project an expected future event
Clear vision, fueled with focused intent

Predictions can and quite often do come true
A very special feeling when predicted by you
It is more powerful when you let no one know
Your prediction is where directed energies flow

Cultivate it, see it and know what you expect
This realization is upon what you singularly reflect
No forceful attention, no coercion of any kind
A quiet visualization projected within your mind

The Universal Language

Prediction is a deliberate act of the will
Upon proper direction every order fulfilled
Impossible for prediction to say no
It must by law flow where directed to go

No such thing as an arbitrary result
Without vision only a prediction assault
Prediction and vision go hand in hand
Unlike an unknown language in a foreign land

Conditions prevail for orders to complete
Unclear, non-specific orders, is predictions defeat
Prevailing conditions exist everywhere
Everything is a prediction, an energy love affair

I Am Only Human

When I say I am only human
From what am I exempt
Justification for half heartedness
What if I refuse to attempt

Much is pitted against me
Race gender appearance and such
Life efforts entails no wind in my sails
Not born with the Midas touch

I am only human
How much I can do
Focused attention and effort
I can't seem to follow through

Why is it so difficult
Can I get the answer from you
Who can I see where they can be
Before my life is through

I try to find the answers
But what does try really mean
No real definition for try
Simply vain efforts unseen

The Universal Language

Being human is no reason
For not fully being yourself
The choices for you seem far too few
There is no one else

When you say I am only human
Know exactly what that means
You are the converging point
Powerfully sustained by the unseen

Ethics / Morality / Integrity

We have been told so many things
Do we know what is actually true
So much opinionated information
What can we possibly do

There is an absolute reality
One we can't misrepresent
This sensitive required information
Is into each heart sent

We pretend not to know its meaning
Ethics, morals and integrity
We always get it right
When asked would I want this for me

Only one rule of engagement
The only one there could ever be
This is the truest form of ethics
The purest form of morals and integrity

Life is one perpetual movement
Possessed by and existing through all
By not honoring our connected oneness
We will miss the collective call

Fortunately missing the call
Is not the forbidden end
Faulty information, misguided steps
Unknowable outcomes upon which we depend

The Universal Language

The universal program is one of order
The program by which all are to thrive
Not the select few living opulently
While others are barely keeping alive

We are all living cells
We are the totality of all that is
We must collectively thrive and prosper
Not just being alive, we are to fully live

We are spirit beings
We are angles, we are god
Only one existing presence
Of which we are all an integral part

We are one existing organism
We all must unify
One consciously existing unit
This we must not deny

Ethics, morals, integrity is the fabrics thread
All are one, one is all no more to be said
One heart, one mind, one sprit yes only one
Failure to heed, human needs no victory won

Words

Words are sentinels
They direct energy's course
Beautiful words create harmony
Harsh words produce force

Some words have no meaning
Some words only empty spaces fill
Some words you can only hear
Some words you actually feel

Descriptions of race and gender
Proclivities of lifestyle
Some words are very new
Some have existed for a while

Some words are very hallowed
Some words not filled with very much
Substance seems to have avoided them
Bereft of the social graces touch

Tattooed word of pain
Thief hoodlum whore
Looking for additional description
Could there be anything more

The Universal Language

Saying it, writing it, or thinking it
Creating is all the same
There are words that heal
There are words that maim

Words can only be descriptive
Not actually the reality
The worst words of all
Are the words that engender
N E G A T I V I T Y

The Message

I am certain there is a message
There is a message everyday
Not paying attention nor making mention
To what your life has to say

I cannot always blame my life on fate
You will always find something on your plate
When viewed reflectively
When ascertaining retrospectively

Some say if I had only known then
Exactly what I know now
I would have already done it
I would already know how

In retrospect as i look over the recent past
I ask myself how long will this uncertainty last
I keep going and going and going
I am always in motion yet never ever knowing

As I internalize uneasy feelings
I ask myself what could this uneasiness be
Ever stressing forward pressing
Is this all that is in store for me

The Universal Language

One idea one break through
Where can my final outcome be
Is this a state of my own choosing
Or was this state chosen for me

Thinking through each passing thought
Going through each passing phase
Is this my long awaited grand finale
Am I just turning another living page

Meticulously turning life's pages
Going laboriously through life's stages
I ask myself what will my conclusion be
As I take a look into life's book,
the message is right in front of me

Chapter 9

The Center

Round and round in circles
Like a cat chasing its tail
Whirling spinning no beginning no ending
Balance starts to fail

When will it stop
When can I get off
Never ending current trending
The all-consuming cost

What do I pay to get away
Resulting dizziness grows every single day
Is this the new order, is this how things are done
Can this possibly be the way for each and everyone

Am I a part of an experiment
Am I immersed in a social plan
How do I find my quiet center
While circling as fast as I can

Can't tell how fast I am going
There are other circlers around me
Sometimes it feels that we are all standing still
Despite accelerated velocity

We are all in some way capable
Capable of stopping the circling trend
Quietly withdraw from group momentum
There is a still quiet center within

The center will avail itself to you
When the center, is centered around your thoughts
Otherwise your efforts compromised
Quiet lessons will still remain to be taught

The Universal Language

On A Rainy Day

Sitting at my open window
Rain falling cleansing the air
Feel the breeze through the trees
You can feel freshness everywhere

I actually love it when it rains
Whether a down pour or a mist
I love it yes, yes, yes I love it
I truly enjoy this

Visiting rainy season locations
Where it rains everyday
Walk outside mouth open wide
Consuming the rain in a natural way

There are electrical ion charges
They are inter- suspended in the air
They evacuate themselves from unnatural locations
But they naturally exist everywhere

When it rains the charges are more active
You take them in with every breath
Were it not for the rain and ion relationship
Breathing might be a matter of life and death

Lovingly sustained by unknown factors
About some we may never ever know
To create immediate naturalness
Perhaps out into the rain you should go

Silhouette / Icon

Silhouette is a shape or an outline
One impressed on the senses and on the mind
The unforgettable silhouettes are the powerful ones
This fully recognizable shape is considered an icon

Forms Shapes and symbols take on meaning
They tend to undeniably reinforce a fact
Without words and without a full explanation
Their symbolic meanings and intentions are intact

Facial shapes and forms can be an icon / silhouette
As in Hitchcock of movie fame
The recognizable shape one never forgets
Identity proceeds it no need to called it by name

Icon / silhouette shapes are created
Was this the plan from the very start
Did they remain focused every single day
Did they from the plan refuse to depart

Was it a dream or a vision to create an icon silhouette
A full frontal daily pursuit having no regrets
Effectively and consciously tasking from day to day
Very clear without fear performing as if at play

The Universal Language

What are you creating do you have a master plan
Prepare and focus the very best that you can
All your efforts create symbols forms and shapes
These are the threads, fabric and fibers of your life-scape

Discipline is a component of the silhouette icon plan
Already having seen the outcome as vividly as you can
Impressing the senses with everything that you do
These components become silhouettes and icons too

There will come a knowing of exactly what to do
Shapes forms and symbols created by you
Fully embellishing the icon silhouette plan
Create your silhouette and icon on demand

You are the silhouette, the icon, and the plan
Who recognizes you? Yes, everyone can
You are the symbol you are the form you are the shape
You are the icon and silhouette you alone did create

Without fore warning, no celebratory adorning
This is the place and point in time of you dawning
Shapes forms and symbols harden into a plan
For what your silhouette and icon will stand

Me

So many places you have gone
So many things you have done
Have you considered effects
Do you feel there are none

Unfortunately, regrettably
This is not actually true
Deliberately or unintentionally
It all comes back to you

Many corroborating conclusions
Why do I act this way
Amidst a haze of confusion
In my defense what can I say

If I apologize and say I'm sorry
Will these effects go away
Am I inclined to find
Resulting effects on another day

When plans don't go as intended
Was this effect created by me
I will find in due time
My indiscretions for all to see

The Universal Language

Do I call myself unlucky
Do I say this is not my day
Do I change do I rearrange
Do I continue this same way

It has come to my attention
That maybe I am to blame
Was it all a result of me
Called by a different name

Commitment

A commitment is an agreement
An agreement with your self
There can also be a commitment
Made to or with someone else

It is actually a promise
Of what you will or will not do
If commitments are promises
One then must follow through

Saying what is convenient
Important issues being evaded
Commitments are black and white
No grey areas nothing shaded

Commitment blended with promise
Equals your intentions as well
Everything that you do
False pretenses to dispel

Reckless actions no forethought
No consequences exist
If this is your final position
Of a true commitment you are remiss

One

Least common denominator
Of all that is
Counting quantifying
The ad infinitum quiz

Many bodies all over the place
How many when tally is done
Each gender and ethnicity
The human race is only one

Do you know every planet
Can you tell me every star
What is the expanse of the Universe
Can you tell me how far

No matter how far
Regardless of how wide
There is only one existence
All components contained inside

So now I ask this question
What can this one body be
A body that contains everything
Which also includes you and me

There are many, many theories
Let's cut right through the chase
The answer is right before you
It is right in front of your face

For some unknown reason
We make this appear very hard
Everything that is
Is within the One Body of God

The Universal Language

One Mind

Flying in formation as birds have always done
Maneuvering aero-dynamically as if they are one
With no external communication as if by design
Could this be for us to see the workings of One Mind

Likewise, fish have this same ability
Turning in flawless unison with perfect agility
In the great fish school, you will also find
They participate and orchestrate with One Mind

As seasons change and leaves begin to fall
Might they too be responding to the One Mind call
In the spring many flowers begin to bloom
This is another version of the one mind tune

Predictable sequences occurring in outer space
The one mind is there it exists in every place
Constellations and yes visits by Halley's Comet
Allows the universe to recite the One Mind Sonnet

Reoccurring exactitude is an undisputed sign
As you might expect this also reflects One Mind
Some underlying messages that we cannot define
Messages pointing to the existence of One Mind

As we search and quest for simple answers
Contemplating answers of the complex kind
The all-pervading conclusive answer is
All that there is, is just One All-Pervading Mind

Brilliance

Brilliance is the cutting edge of excellence
Excellence is that which is highly refined
Brilliance and excellent are interactions
The culmination of the brain and mind

What is the most profound difference
Between the brain and the mind
The brain is biological and physical
Mind is spirit of the rarified kind

Everything that is accomplished
Is fundamentally a physical task
Force of habit disciplined focus
Sometimes asking how long will this last

Should you be fortunate
If brilliance should grant you a peek
Maybe soon but never right away
Brilliance may reveal what you seek

A fleeting glimmer of brilliance
Just of what brilliance is comprised
Brilliance all too frequently escapes many
Most especially the one who only tries

The Universal Language

Try has no established definition
No definition or meaning at all
You will or you will not embrace brilliance
Otherwise you cannot heed the brilliance call

There are many and varied strategies
What can I do for brilliance to find
Keep brilliance upper most in your brain
Until brilliance converts into pure mind

External

On the outside looking in
Upon which point can you depend
Do you think its greener on the other side
Or is this a cliché behind which to hide

Looking at people and places far away
I want to live like them and do as they
Pictures and poses looking their best
Can poses and snapchats replicate stress

Looking for the sexiest representation of me
Long hair butterfly lashes looks so naturally
As I look into the mirror with eyes open wide
I ask myself what is really and truly inside

Not pretty, not sexy, not so very slim
Being all that I can be the outlook seems grim
There is within you a pure and natural self
It is not possible to find what you seek anywhere else

Searching and looking may imply a location outside
This is not true no need to open eyes too wide
For what you are seeking you will be the first who knows
No external requirement you can see it with eyes close

Dash

Date of birth, date of death
A dash separates the first and final breath
The dash represents an account to give
Very much alive yet some never ever live

The dash is so very important
The space between birth and death
Either fleeting or protracted
Did I give it my very best

Is my life memorable
Is it an undiscernible blip on the screen
Is this my true intention
Is this what I really mean

When under observation
Without the option of words
Would you understand my intentions
Would my life seem absurd

Have I been a good human being
Have I been a good friend
Do I honor my word
Can you upon me depend

SpiritMan

Can you believe me
When I say I have your back
Would it be doubtful
Is my dependability under attack

Live truly and honestly every single day
Accentuate your dash as you go along your way
There was a beginning and the will be an end
Only the dash is upon which you can depend

On making the final approach
When you feel that you are through
Only one question remains
What kind of dash were you

(Inspired by Lisa Nichols)

The Universal Language

Love is the universal language
When you Love it becomes first language to you
It is the only language known from the very start
By heart all the way through

Oh, so very easy to learn, you can't get it wrong
As soon as you Love, the more Love becomes strong
Strong Love is the magnetism that causes all things to be
It causes everything; it is the cause of you, it is the cause of me

We are to teach the language of Love to others, teach it to one and to all
It is our individual commission to answer to this noble, global call
We are to live Love and we are to give Love, everywhere that we go
Each day just say, I Love you to someone that you think you don't know

As you share the language of Love with others as you go along your way
You will have implanted a seed in them that grows and grows, everyday
They then will know the language of Love; they too will begin to share
Soon we will find the language of Love being spoken everywhere

When we all speak a common language, when intentions are understood
The result will be for all concerned to experience only that which is good
There is no requirement for money, there is nothing we cannot do
The only required components are simply, Love and me and you

So, let's make the language of Love
The most common language spoken on Planet Earth
Very soon there will come a point in time,
You will see its value and know it's worth

There will be no more hunger and suffering
For some neglected unfortunate few
The language Love also teaches what happens to others
Also happens to you………

About the Author

SpiritMan formerly known as Benjamin Martin is a Spiritual / Metaphysical Writer, A Master Performing Poet, Philosopher, Environmentalist, Humanitarian and Pianist.

He attended Allen University in South Carolina majoring in English. He also attended Florida A & M University in Tallahassee, Florida as a Speech and Theatre major. SpiritMan is presently enrolled in the doctoral program at University of Metaphysical Sciences in Arcata, California. SpiritMan has lived in West Africa and in the Caribbean. SpiritMan is a native of St. Petersburg, Florida and currently resides in Atlanta, Georgia.

The commission on the life of SpiritMan is to promote Human Compassion and Unconditional Love on Planet Earth through his Discourses, Poetry, Workshops, Love Fest Events, School Engagements, and Various Personal Appearances.

For more information visit the SpiritMan website at www.spiritman222.com.